D0924159

Downloading a Friendly Universe

Book 1

Your Presence is Requested

Elke Siller Macartney

BOOK PUBLISHERS NETWORK

Book Publishers Network
P.O. Box 2256
Bothell • WA • 98041
PH • 425-483-3040
www.bookpublishersnetwork.com

Copyright © 2010 by **© 2010 Elke Siller Macartney**
www.DownloadingaFriendlyUniverse.com
All rights reserved. No part of this book may be reproduced, stored
in, or introduced into a retrieval system, or transmitted in any form,
or by any means (electronic, mechanical, photocopying, recording, or
otherwise) without the prior written permission of the publisher.

10 9 8 7 6 5 4 3 2 1

Printed in the United States of America

LCCN 2010908050
ISBN10 1-935359-38-X
ISBN13 978-1-935359-38-8

Proofreader: Julie Scandora
Cover designer: Nina Barnett
Cover art: Alexandria Odjonii
Typographer: Stephanie Martindale

Downloading A Friendly Universe honors and celebrates the natural forces of the human experience: love, creation, destruction and essence; and reassures us that our state of consciousness in which these forces dance never dies.

We have free will to use these forces to create our own direction with open hearts or closed minds. *Downloading A Friendly Universe* challenges us to live rooted in our essence with openness and compassion for fellow humans as they play out their own lives. This is certainly a more graceful way to live.

John Caskey, M.D., Santa Fe, New Mexico

Downloading a Friendly Universe is a welcome twenty-first century guide on how (if we wish) to recreate our lives and therefore our world. It provides insight on reclaiming our true selves (an expanded version of how we usually define you and me) and the seeds for how to take action. It is not meant to be read in one sitting, though you may choose to do so, but to be kept always at hand.

Keep it near you, as I do, to serve as inspiration on your journey- a constant reminder of your true nature and your power to bring forth change even in seemingly perilous times.

Deirdre C. Grimes, mother, designer, nurse and spiritual seeker

I am still 'downloading' from the downloads! I am simply vibrating!

Alexandra Odjonii, cover artist for Downloading a Friendly Universe, Paris/Seattle

Downloading a Friendly Universe wraps around me like a cozy, silky soft eiderdown on a cold Winter night. The energy that comes through is so incredibly gentle and so very loving. It, to me, carries some of what I sense from the writings of Byron Katy and Eckart Tolle. There is a deeper gentleness and palatable feeling of pure love.

I absolutely love it.

I enjoy savoring this precious resource. I don't want to dash through it. I find I read a little and just feel the energy of it swirl around me in a delightful embrace.

I would definitely recommend it. It is definitely good information to study, feel and ponder. I want more!

Cassie Hepburn, healer, Langley, BC, Canada

This lively and engaging collaboration by Elke Macartney and the Friendly Universe is well-written, clear and direct. They call us to remember who we are as spirited human beings and to take courage to trust in our own capacity to live a life on this planet as though living in a friendly universe.

Each download reveals a sensitivity to how humans learn, providing a meta-narrative that loops back to bring in previously established points, thus helpfully integrating and connecting the four emphases that conceptually ground the book: four forces of consciousness, our awakening to this consciousness, and reminding us of the way we can and do participate in creating the world in which we all dwell.

Kathleen D. Clark, Ph.D., spiritual director,
associate professor, School of Communication,
University of Akron, Akron, OH

Elke's diligent Downloads gently and lovingly remind us to connect with our Higher Selves and, most importantly, to experience the eternal peace that comes when embracing life from this perspective.

I chose to use "diligent" to describe this work because I think the following definitions of "diligent" definitely apply to the Downloads:

1. constant in effort to accomplish something

2. done or pursued with persevering attention

Belle Harrell, Ph.D. teacher, Georgia, USA and New Zealand

With simplicity, startling insights and immense compassion, Elke shares in her new book the voices of our collective higher selves, reflecting back to us the wisdom embedded deep within everyone and available to all. Weaving the voice of this book into the growing chorus of those inviting us to awaken to our highest and best selves, Elke makes a powerful contribution to the tradition of messengers reminding us and reawakening us to what we already know—Love is the foundation for everything.

Bobbye Middendorf, The Write Synergies Guru, Chicago, IL
http://www.writesynergiescopywriting.com

Everything *Downloading a Friendly Universe* touches is energized by a special vibration that is hard to describe. I pick it up, I open to the words, and something wonderful takes place: I am empowered to be me.

Rev. Tony Dellapenna, Ashland, Oregon

In trying to come up with something to say about *DAFU*, it's hard to come up with anything as the words stand so perfectly on their own. This is the honest advice that each of us is hoping someone will tell us and here it is- we're telling ourselves!

If you have any interest in what your subconscious might say to you, *DAFU* is for you.

Alex Bjorn McDonald
human being, festival creator, Washington

Elke has touched, in powerful ways, the lives of many individual lives throughout her career as author, intuitive, wise woman and soccer mom. She has profoundly affected and helped me to improve my life! Through this book she is bringing to us teachings and assurances that we, the human family, desperately need during a time of incredible change and uncertainty. Thank you Elke!

Marcie Oliver, business owner, Redmond, Washington

Through these amazing downloads, Elke heralds an imminent and positive change towards a well-balanced universe. Guess what, you have a major role to play in this change and you get to write your own part. Downloading a Friendly Universe prepares you not only for the performance of your life but also for a lifetime of performance. The world will be a better place if you read it.

P. Armitage, adventure philanthropist, British Isles

I dedicate this book to the downloaders everywhere. You know you are a downloader if: You are a dreamer. You care enough to share your gifts in any way you can. You see opportunity in the obstacles. You know who you are: a bright Spirit inhabiting an amazing Human experience.

Shine on.

Contents

Foreword

In trying to come up with something to say *about Downloading a Friendly Universe* (*DAFU*), it's hard to come up with anything as the words stand so perfectly on their own. People's unique approaches to life give them each a different perspective and something to take away from what they have to say. Of course, there is no "they" as we are speaking to ourselves. This is the honest advice that each of us is hoping someone will tell us, and here it is—we're telling ourselves!

Every time I pick up *DAFU* I end up speechless. It shuts up everything we can come up with as an excuse, and not with some damning power but with a much needed reminder that this whole game we've got going on is us.

Many channeled books contain all sorts of wild numbers and information on various dimensions and somewhat mindboggling evidence. The beautiful thing about *DAFU* is that it's like an artistic masterpiece: it can be picked apart and studied to the nth degree, or it can stand as a surface-level positive-reinforcement read. If you have any interest in what your subconscious might say to you, *DAFU* is for you.

In an attempt to come up with some sort of review on *DAFU*, I haven't seemed to find the words that capture how I feel about it. On the other hand, when I let myself go in a free write, similar to how I imagine your downloads to feel, another voice steps in, and even then typing gets hard, as I just want to listen—but here is what wants to be said:

DAFU is the honest conversation each of us needs to have. Snapping out of "The Game" and taking a serious look at the whos, whats, and hows of life is the next step for the human race. *DAFU* is the canary in the coalmine for all of us. Listen to what we have to say to ourselves: This isn't coming from an outside source or a different over-mind…we are talking to ourselves! What an amazing opportunity! No matter your race, color, or creed; monetary status or lack thereof; religious, political, moral, or world views, the words contained within *DAFU* speak to us because they are from us!

Like a drink of water for a parched throat, a jumpstart for a dead battery, nourishment for the hungry belly, *DAFU* gives you and me the needed kick at exactly the right moment to get us going again.

Just as *DAFU* confirms, humanity is at a very interesting point in the grand scheme of things. We've created our part in all that is around us, now it's time to fess up to our mess. Like a much needed mentor's words, *DAFU* provides its readers with words that unite us as a whole—not just humanity but all of life—and still separates each individual and reminds us each that responsibility lies within us, not outside in a government, economy, police force. We can't even blame the other individual as you are me and I am you!

We are waking up to our divine purpose and right to exist as a much prided leaf on the tree of God. Being born in human form is an honor and no easy task. I like to imagine that there is a waiting line on the other side just for the opportunity to be a part of the epic race that millions of sperm make on their way to the egg. When sperm meets egg, that spark that becomes a life is the one in a million. When you were a child and mother told you that you were so special, she was right. Congratulations human! You've made it! Now that we've made it this far, what are we racing for? The race was over the minute sperm reached egg. From then on, nature has pretty much taken over. Now the race is over, and it's time to enjoy the victory—will you be a pompous, unsatisfied winner, gloating that you are the greatest and continue your competition to the top of some egoic mountain that doesn't exist? Or will you realize that competition is nothing more than a way of helping the whole by creating a reason to push on?

As mentioned before, you are me and I am you, and without separation, how could there be a winner and a loser? There simply *is*. And then in our dualistic, human mind we create a negative and positive, and thus a winner and loser.

In the race of life, *DAFU* is a nudge in the right direction. It's a last minute reminder that you have a job interview shortly, or it's the coach's advice that kicks the team into gear not a moment too soon; or it's a drink of water for a thirsty marathon runner.

Every time I start to write a review or whatever it is I'm trying to come up with, it seems that before I know it, I've moved my energy towards my passion—anything to do with festivals. Whether it's sewing some new costume, researching local bands to book for upcoming events, practicing wicked dance moves, whatever—anything related to *DAFU* inspires on an unstoppable level. Much as eating a healthy meal or drinking fresh-squeezed juice satisfies the body, reading *DAFU* satisfies the soul. *DAFU* inspires me to live my purpose in every moment of existence.

This isn't a book that says you need to change or even shift perspectives in order to relate to your unique outlook. Whatever line of thought you chose to follow in life, *DAFU* provides a firm but gentle nudge in not the "right" direction, but YOUR direction. Just as gas stoves have a pilot light continually burning and ready to light the oven up, each human has a "purpose-light" burning and willing to light up the entire being if only we turn up the flame. Since each oven is our own, no one else can turn up the heat but each of us. There are many ways to warm up the oven: meditation, exercise, education, etc. Yet, *DAFU* is one of the guaranteed ways to help turn up your internal pilot light.

Among all traditions and lines of thought, humans are and the earth itself is shifting and coming to a changing point. How we label that shift comes in many forms, but that we all see it happening seems a fair assumption to make. As we move into novel fields of consciousness, words like those presented in *DAFU* are gold to anyone riding the wave of change on the planet.

Alex Bjorn McDonald, human being, festival creator
Washington State. USA

Author's note:

The preceding inspirational words came sailing into my inbox from a young friend of mine, a 22 year old person who understood the importance and the influence of the downloads right away…even before he read the book! I was so overwhelmed by the power of his words; I decided they needed to be shared.

While our culture does not acknowledge this, and most certainly our institutions do not support them, a different kind of human being has arrived in the world. As a group consciousness, they've already changed everything. Highly intuitive, creative, and hard to pin down, these now young adults are here to break down stereotypes and walls, create new ways of communicating (instant messaging anyone?), and whole new ways of being we are not even aware of…yet.

Prepare yourselves! Time for a change. People like my friend Alex are awake and not willing to go to sleep.

Acknowledgement

This book (and the subsequent books in the series) was made possible through willingness: Both my willingness to receive the words for you to study and enjoy, and the willingness of others who saw the profound value in getting the downloads out to you. With limited resources, yet with willing hearts, my husband Jim and I knew we were working with something extraordinary. So my first tearful thank you is to you, dearest James Macartney: You were present for all of the downloads as they were happening. You held the space for Spirit to enter in; you gently asked questions of the voices coming through; you were a fellow explorer of this Friendly Universe. You were the first to even suggest I had a book in the making. While I assumed these powerful conversations were for our use only, you knew this was to be shared with the world.

Jim my dear, despite your extreme effort in writing your own incredible book, *Crisis to Creation*, while I was putting together this book, you still had time to cheer me on, dry my tears when I harbored doubts and fears, and support me in every way possible. This book would still be an idea without you. You brought it to life! I love you.

As mentioned, this was put together with limited economic resources, yet plentiful people resources. A *Downloading* team stepped forward to make it happen:

Barbro Rakos transcribed the downloads from the original voice recordings. A brilliant visionary with a full, busy life, she stepped right in when I asked for help. Barbro dear, you energized the words with your insights and comments on the downloads. You were always as excited as I was to hear of a "new" arrival. Your attitude shored me up when I wondered if this was going to happen, your creative ideas made me smile with joy. You will forever be ensconced in the Hall of Fate: You knew this was to be. Thank you.

Leila Dawn Anasazi is an extraordinarily gifted writer and blogger and all around artist. Your roles were many, Leila, but mostly I thank you for your empowering words at the very onset of my seeing a book in here: You said: "This is powerful stuff, you know." It was all I needed to hear from a woman I deeply respect.

Valerie Kovacs Kraft is the kind of friend everyone should have, yet I know that a friend like her is rare. I don't even know how to thank you, Valerie, for hours and hours of talking this through, for checking up on me, for your honest appraisal of my first attempts to put some sort of order to this work. Thank you for your undying, unconditional support. I love you because you are always your true self. And that calls out my true self.

Judith Sult, marketing maven, wise woman, sage…this woman was my advisor and kept me going with her unconditional support. Judith, thank you for saying: "This work is a success because you're treating it very differently from other projects that were less so." When I asked why, you stated, "Because you are creating it step by step; you are present, you are following Spirit impeccably." How can I possibly *not* succeed with wisdom like this?

Over my lifetime as a dreamer, my parents Ingeborg Siller and Walter Siller saw to it the dreamer was safe and free to dream. Thank you, mom and dad.

In my life as a mom to two now young men, I was so fortunate that they never questioned my interesting, out-of-the-box work and journey....well, at least not out loud! Ryan and Eron, I wrote this book for you guys. This is your present and future I am championing here. Create your lives with love and care and do not ever, ever leave your dreams behind. I am so glad you showed up...right in the nick of time.

Others too many to name have held forth at different crucial times:

Thanks to John Caskey and Deirdre Grimes for the use of their home to retreat to when I actually took the collection of downloads and put them into a book form.

Thanks to Marcie Oliver who took the book apart, and download by download, put it in the best order—the order you see now.

Thanks to publisher Sheryn Hara of Book Publishers Network: You listen, you bring order to chaos, you shepherd, you are the best!

I am missing some folks, I know, but please know I am grateful for my fellow downloaders out there. You all keep the dream of a world where well-being is the "bottom line" alive.

I am so grateful. I am so blessed.

Elke

It is us talking with us.

Introduction

This is a book about our perception: how we view life and death and the planet and the universe ... everything. What we perceive determines the way we treat our everyday lives, each other, and the world. As suggested in one of the chapters: "Life, all of life, is a perception."

I am fascinated by how we perceive things. Why do we have such a variety of viewpoints on everything from religion and the nature of the universe to our everyday politics to the way we care for each other and the planet...or don't care? *Downloading a Friendly Universe* offers up some answers to the nature of our perceptions. And the answers are coming from an incredibly powerful, yet intriguingly familiar source.

The following "downloaded" messages come from a "Friendly Universe," a group voice with a great deal of interest in our human journey. Yet they have no hidden agenda. Their discussion of our perceptions is well summarized by words attributed to physicist Albert Einstein: When asked, "What, in your opinion is the most important question facing humanity today?" Einstein replied:

I think the most important question facing humanity is, "Is the universe a friendly place?" This is the first and most basic question all people must answer for themselves.

For if we decide that the universe is an unfriendly place, then we will use our technology, our scientific discoveries and our natural resources to achieve safety and power by creating bigger walls to keep out the unfriendliness, and bigger weapons to destroy all that which is unfriendly. I believe that we are getting to a place where technology is powerful enough that we may either completely isolate or destroy ourselves as well in this process.

If we decide that the universe is neither friendly nor unfriendly and that God is essentially "playing dice with the universe," then we are simply victims to the random toss of the dice, and our lives have no real purpose or meaning.

But if we decide that the universe is a friendly place, then we will use our technology, our scientific discoveries, and our natural resources to create tools and models for understanding that universe. Because power and safety will come through understanding its workings and its motives.

Downloading a Friendly Universe states as much, suggesting we presently perceive ourselves at the mercy of a less-than-friendly universe. Therefore, we see our lives through the lens of unbalanced destruction and the defense against that destruction—a non-ending battle we seem to be rather addicted to. Just listen to the news, no matter where you are: Isn't it usually about what is being destroyed or what we are at war with or what we are defending? The voices from a Friendly Universe are asking us to wake up from the trance of destruction and defense in order to create our lives from a new, more rewarding perception.

Who Is the Voice Behind the Downloads?

The best way I can describe what or who is bringing through these compassionate "downloads" (as I came to call them) is as follows: **It is us speaking to us.** "They" are a collective of our true selves, the "being" part of the human being, also known as our observers or our spirits. This collection of our selves includes our future generations. What a comforting thought: We actually have a future!

The downloads arrive by my speaking into a digital recorder, and out comes a profound message. I always keep my recorder handy for the times a new download is transmitted. I've downloaded while sitting on the sofa with my husband or while in a café or on a hike. I then collect the downloads, have them transcribed, and edit them for clarity. This book is the first collection in a series of five—so there are more being downloaded on a regular basis. We apparently have a lot to say to us!

What Are the Downloads About?

There are key concepts expanded upon in *Downloading a Friendly Universe*:

- We live in a conscious and attentive Universe.
- The basis of the Universe is Consciousness.
- There are Four Forces of Consciousness: Creation, Destruction, Love, and Essence.
- We are awakening to our awareness of the Four Forces of Consciousness.

The downloads also elaborate on essential wisdom we can all use:

- We live on a free-will planet. What we create is up to us.
- As we awaken to our creative power, we will see how we often create unbalanced destruction and the defense against that destruction. There is no judgment about this.

- As we awaken, we will create from an intention of well-being and balance. There is no judgment about this either.

- We are in a unique position to take advantage of an opportunity to create a world of balance and well-being.

- It's all up to us. What will we create?

What the Downloads Ask of You and Me

- Try out the concepts and perspectives in the downloads for yourself. There is no need to believe any of it. The downloads are either self-evident, or not.

- There are very few cultural references in the downloads. They are meant for people everywhere. No matter if you live in an apartment, a home with a dirt floor or stone or carpet, a military barrack, a prison, or a mansion—no matter who you are or where you live, the downloads are for everyone to study, enjoy, ponder, discuss, utilize, agree with, disagree with, and experience.

- The downloads have no hidden agendas or dogma, so you do not have to ditch your current belief system or spiritual tradition.

- Listen with your heart and mind.

- Be discerning.

- Enjoy the journey.

Final Note

Some of the downloads include questions from friends or my husband or me. For clarity, those questions and ponderings are summed up and written in *italics* in the text.

As representatives of a friendly universe, we have no particular need for you to change anything. Simply put, we have no needs. Interestingly enough, though, we do have a desire ... for the human to fully express his or her potential.

Chapter 1

Who Is a Friendly Universe?

You may be wondering why we strongly suggest you term this compilation of discussions *Downloading a Friendly Universe.* Just who is this friendly Universe, anyway?

The term "friendly Universe" implies, of course, that there may be an unfriendly universe as well, for that is what the human mind does. It hears one thing or it perceives one thing—a term, say, or a picture or an idea—and almost immediately brings to its attention the opposite. Therefore, for every positive action one takes, a human usually believes that the positive action is denying a negative action to occur. For every positive thought, the same can be said. Humans live in duality—and so you often support and energize that which you do not necessarily wish to create. For example, do the great majority of humans truly wish to create war situations? Or terror, poverty, disease, and starvation? Within the grand majority of hearts on this planet, the answer is no, this is not the desire of most humans—even those born into these circumstances.

Within their hearts and within their essences, there is a knowing that there is an energy which somehow affirms something else!

The energy we call *a friendly Universe* affirms the following:

Consciousness is the basis of the Universe; it is the elemental element of creation in the Universe. All that is created from Consciousness, all that is destroyed with Consciousness, all that draws its life and breath through the love of Consciousness, all that comes into form because of its essential nature in Consciousness—the all-in-all *is* Consciousness with a desire to create.

Can you see how friendly this is? Can you see how at its heart, Consciousness is the basis of a friendly Universe? By friendly we mean *accepting of all*. It's a non-judgmental friendship. As representatives of a friendly Universe, we have no particular need for you to change anything. Simply stated, we have no needs. Interestingly enough though, we do have a desire: Our desire is for the human to express fully his or her potential. Another way of stating this is we have the desire for each and every human to be about the daily activity of expressing his or her essence.

So downloading and bringing into form these discussions from a friendly Universe supports all life-forms expressing themselves boldly, with clarity, and with no obstruction to their own essence.

This is the essence of friendship we offer you with no other hidden agendas. None. Naturally there will be some who will read that last statement and be suspicious. Surely, there is a hidden intent within these downloads. Perhaps there are what you would call "evil forces" at play here, wishing to lull people into a state of unconditional love, just so something conditional can be sprung upon them! And yet we state that all actions you take which bring into existence unnecessary and mostly unwanted creations, such as war, poverty, disease, etc., are acceptable to us as well because we accept all. That is our friendship with you.

No matter what, our desires are for you to express your essence, as we are doing our very best to express ours.

So in this moment, we would like to share a love story.

One of the many, many, many manifestations of a universal Consciousness has been living forms who draw breath, have a life span, and within that life span, have an opportunity to affect other life-forms in quite a powerful way. These entities who draw breath also have a profound effect on a special planet. They are some of the most beloved entities ever created by a conscious Universe.

These unique entities came into being because of a desire to experience a separation from the parent source of Consciousness. And why would there be such desire?

Because of the universal, infinite, and timeless desires of Love.

The force of Love created creations which could create in and of themselves. Love created creations that could destroy. Love created creations that would draw breath and, even in so doing, affect the whole of any particular planetary system. It was a grand and loving experiment in Creation.

The opportunities and potentials of this experiment in separation and creation were infinite in scope. And so the love story is this: Within all societies, all cultures, every single group of people—whether it's a group of two or into the billions—the seeds of love are at their core, and the desire to express love is there.

You may wonder how this could be when there are so many people who express in hateful, revengeful, ornery, horrible, and terrifying ways. Well, within each human being there is a core of love. If there is a core of love, then each is expressing love in his or her own way. For every act of terror, for every act of anger, for every action that you might frown upon, there is a cry for love and a desire for love.

Every person on the planet does not operate in a vacuum, no matter how isolated the person is. For every single person on the planet affects the whole planet. Every person is also affected by the thought-forms, the consciousness, of the whole planet. Some people are affected in ways that are overwhelming to those people. They feel the energy of the collective thought-forms and consciousness, and they feel burdened by this. Then there are those who also feel they are stuck in a life they do not desire, a life of lack of resources, and a life which is cold and empty, or overwhelming and exhausting. So their cry for love will be in ways which try to break out of those stuck places and undesirable lives. Perhaps some of them may even be called terrorists in their lifetimes or revolutionaries or soldiers or visionaries or any number of names and roles.

There are also some who are born into societies where there is an abundance of resources and an abundance of opportunity. And yet, they take the opportunities and discount them, creating lives of quiet or noisy desperation. They do not allow themselves to express fully because they, too, are feeling the fears operating within the mass consciousness.

Seeded within both groups—those who are born without much and those who are born with much to be grateful for—is the gentle and unconditional power of Love.

It is important for each and every human being to tap into the force of Love, and see within their greater potential how that Love is to be expressed. Why so important? May we remind you there would be no humans on the planet right now if Love did not eventually prevail. It would be impossible for humans to be in existence because time and time again there have been opportunities for mass extinguishing events within whole societies.

In the history of the planet, and up to this day, whenever many people are extinguished through the destructive forces gone rampant (via tsunamis, hurricanes, volcanic explosions, man-made disasters, pandemics, and so forth), there is opportunity for a more massive extinguishing of humans. As you know, these opportunities have been many-fold. And yet the prevailing Love Force calls people back into creation. Love calls to humanity and says, "Come back to the planet. Come join a friendly Universe and create your dreams and desires yet again."

So the love story is this: Humanity has freely chosen to create whatever it has created in the past, and it can choose again in every moment. Every moment. There is no one overriding entity saying to humanity, "No you can't. You can only create further destruction; you can only create further strife, for that is the essential human."

Yet, for some reason, even though Love allowed the potential of humans to express their true essence as divine beings of Love and Creation, humans have, instead, persisted in your habituation and addiction to drama, to strife, and to "This might be good now, but it's not going to last."

Note how when there are peacetimes in your societies—including the very society you live in—that moment of peacetime is brief. It is in peacetimes when your mass consciousness does not trust that peace can endure. So you create war—again and again.

Thus, we can see how one would be skeptical of the very term "friendly" Universe. You may wonder, perhaps this is a euphemism of some kind, such as "friendly fire," a term used for when one soldier falls because his "friends," or comrades, actually shot at him. We are not shooting at you. We are simply bringing to you the desire that is seeded within you, helping to stir that awake. We are here to awaken the seeds of love and well-being in every person and every society on the planet.

We have no other agenda than this.

So we suggest you do not isolate yourself any further as a society or as a human individual. Go into the silence of meditation or prayer, and tap into Love. Then connect with every human being on this planet of choice. Even when you're not in prayer or meditation, connect with the other living beings as you wander through your days. Honor them. See them. Really and truly notice them. See the love there, even in those who are angry, distraught, or perhaps mentally or psychically unstable. See Love there, and notice what happens. We are not saying there will be an overnight turnaround of society to one of well-being; nor are we saying every human will transform his or her habituation to drama right away.

Still, if you do not acknowledge and honor the seeds of Love in others, then the habituation to destruction and drama will stick around for much longer than necessary. If no attempts are made to reach out of your isolation to your fellow co-creators, then promoting well-being will not easily become the new habit.

Back to the initial question, "Just who is this friendly Universe?" We would like you to keep your curiosity alive. We suggest you be discerning people, and we have a desire for that discernment to apply to any of the words stated here, or in any other discussion you might have with any consciousness which describes itself as separate from human consciousness.

We wish to state, though, we are not separate from human consciousness. We are created from the desires of human consciousness to enliven the seeds of Love. So we are a mass Consciousness as well, coming to you within the human context of these downloads. As a friendly Universe, we are an energy which tunes into the dreams and the desires of human consciousness.

Human consciousness has been left to its own devices for a very long time now. As such, humans have created varying forms of well-being and non-well-being. Now however, the human as Consciousness-in-form desires something else: to create a planet that has as its focus well-being for all the forms of consciousness on the planet.

As a friendly Universe we support this. We have been created by your thoughts, and as long as you continue to support a friendly link between Universe and human, we will continue to exist.

I'm just wondering for myself how it is I can download these tre-mendously supportive messages, and yet, I don't think a day goes by when I doubt it all—and I mean all of it. I have a connection to you, and I know you exist, but I have a terror, just as you've stated: What if there is something hiding here that's awful and evil and will consume me and everybody else? How can all of this exist within this one puny human? I know we have tremendous potential, and I can see this in people's eyes and actions. But I also see their persistent habituation to destruction. It just seems like a non-ending battle of polar opposites.

Well friendly Universe, do you have something to say about this?

You are free to work with both creation and destruction. It takes both to have a life.

As to how this all exists within one puny human, we say the follow-ing: All the humans who have ever made a powerful impression on this planet by challenging the status quo with a new way of thinking, acting, and being have harbored doubt within their hearts. They harbored the belief that your habituation to destruction and drama will continue, no matter what they said, no matter what they did, no matter what they believed, no matter what they created. There isn't a human on the planet who doesn't also harbor this doubt: that the change they envision has its opposite, right there, standing close, ready to pounce and snuff out whatever light they produce, whatever idea they wish to manifest.

Because of this fear, which is rampant upon the planet, you have amped up the opportunities to heal this fear—if you can but see this.

We understand how painful this process is because, after all, we as a friendly Universe are created by your thought-forms. So we understand the pain which a conscious awakening can bring. Yet we also understand the delight when, upon awakening from the nightmare, you understand it was simply a nightmare—a literal figment of your imagination, created by your fertile minds.

If you're in the art of moviemaking, you can create audio-visual nightmares for people to witness and feel they are a part of. Similarly, you can also create a reality which furthers the nightmare of doubting a friendly Universe—and of doubting the Love Force.

We ask you to consider this: Could you hold for one day, one twenty-four-hour period, that you have the potential to change the world for the positive through your actions on that day?

And then could you act from that?

Could you do this without fear and doubt stalking your thoughts?

Well, we do not have the answer to this—but perhaps you can give it a try! For one day, no matter what activities you have in that day and whether you are at work or at play or raising a family or acting alone and whether you are planting seeds or chopping down a tree—whatever it is you are actually up to in any one day—could you see the day as having the potential to bring well-being to the planet—permanently?

How would you act on that one day? If you were to declare today as the day to change the world, what would you do? Who would you speak to? What activities would you participate in? Would you sit in meditation for a greater part of the day? Would you act and bring love to a lonely person? Would you be kind to an animal? Would you download some thoughts from a friendly Universe?

Give it a try and see. What would you do in that day? And let us know the results. Of course, you will let us know the results—because we are you! We are created by your thoughts. We are here to challenge each of you to ask of yourselves: "Can I adopt a new habit of creating from my desire for well-being? How can I express the love within me?"

We look forward to your report. And we look forward to reporting to you how we love you infinitely and forever.

That is all for now.

You are not fallen angels; you are specially created angels, fully adaptable to life on a living planet.

Chapter 2

Arrival and Presence

This is a lesson in arrival and presence.

The human beings have had their share of times when there was barely a person home in the body because they felt too much and saw too much, yet were asleep to the possibilities of being human. And then there've been times when certain persons were quite present, quite aware of their body as a piece of the whole earth-body, including within the ecosystem of the earth-body location they resided in. In other words, they knew they were a part of the whole and were also aware that their personal body was a holistic ecosystem.

For a number of centuries, your presence in a body has been viewed as something to be dealt with as if one were dealing with a scourge: the scourge of being born into a body. There has been an emphasis on the separation of body from its inhabiting soul (or being). From this view, many diseases have been collected and stored in the human form. How sad to perceive oneself as a scourge, as a curse, rather than as an uplifting presence. Is it any wonder that humans have treated the planet as the scourge of cancer would treat the body? This perception is so ingrained in the majority of humans; you will find reference to humans as a curse in religious traditions all over the earth. Hence the concept of original sin, and also hence the concept that to be born into a body is to be endured rather than enjoyed.

The truth is there is a miracle on the planet, well loved by Creation, called the human being. Human beings are bridging agents between the material plane of existence and the higher frequency planes or dimensions. There are other life-forms in those higher frequencies, but on this earth there has never been a life-form with such a fascinating evolutionary path: to be firmly placed within materiality while still possessing the potential to transcend that materiality.

All life-forms have concurrent frequencies which are material and immaterial. All living forms therefore have frequencies which can be measured on the material plane by humans via the machinery of the five senses, as well as the internal mechanisms to explore *beyond* the five senses. Awareness practices such as the disciplines of meditation, in-tuning, prayer, contemplation, and journeying facilitate such explorations.

One can also discern frequencies of living forms with gifts rather elusive to some—for instance some people see or sense energies or hear inter-dimensional frequencies. Yet, might we suggest that practice makes for a perfect awareness of these frequencies. Should humanity choose to evolve out of its pattern of individuals viewing themselves as a cancer or scourge or sin; so too will their future evolve, and the utilization of intuitive practices will happily intersect with their everyday lives.

This is a shift from perceiving humans as small, angry, hurt victims of a great Fall to perceiving human beings as potential, a light, a blessing, an integral part of the whole, well loved, quite blessed by Creation. See your collective selves as spiritual beings integrated into a collection of material selves. You are not fallen angels; you are specially created angels fully adaptable to life on a living planet. Today, in this phase of your evolution, you are only partially conscious of your potential.

Seeing yourselves as small, silly, insignificant, and unable to do anything of worth is the greatest lie humanity has ever conceived, believed, and locked into. You've been caught up in this scenario for so long that you are completely unaware of the lie. Your predominant waking consciousness has been this limited and stunted perception. Meanwhile, in your dreams and visions and imagination, you've always known you are so much more.

The trick at play here is the trance of amnesia—self-amnesia. You are playing out the ultimate in forgetfulness. In your collective forgetfulness, you've even allowed an illness in forgetfulness to take hold in your wisdom-elder years. So-named Alzheimer's disease is merely a reflection of how trivialized you have made wisdom. In indigenous cultures, there is a tradition of honoring and accepting as a noble truth the wisdom of the elders. Now, however, elders are seen not as a vessel of wisdom ready to pour into society's creations, but as empty vessels with nothing to offer. The truth is, from birth, you are built to be vessels of wisdom, inspiration, vision. This is truly who you are if you were to remember: wisdom-keepers, en-visionaries, creators—the being in human form.

Some of your children are born remembering who they are, and they are refusing to forget. This is why so many of them are a challenge to the status quo, because the status quo is stuck in the groove of enslavement to the idea of puny and sinful. The children are not buying it. And before you all lose both their wisdom and the elders' wisdom, it is time you consider a grand wake-up call the likes of which this earth has never seen.

The wake-up call is this: Creation is calling upon you to remember your true nature as powerful beings involved in a divine Plan. The Plan includes forgetting who you are, so that you may make the "return trip" to your remembrance—stronger in your purpose, mature in your collective wisdom. It is time to no longer play small; but humbly, compassionately play—full out—your divine role. The closer your actions are to your divine purpose, the more you each will see yourselves as a delight on the earth, a blessing, a steward, a healing presence, rather than a scourge.

Let's heal this misunderstanding. Allow yourselves to be a blessing in your lives. Start revealing your innate gifts, and then move on to share those gifts with others. Be your self full out, and all will be blessed for it.

And that is all for now.

So breathe and know this: All of this is Consciousness.
You live in a world which shapes itself around you.

Chapter 3

Welcome to a Conscious Universe

Welcome to a conscious Universe. This is the very world you sit upon or stand in, lie down on, run through, play with, are born into and die into. You expand and grow here. You contract and disappear here.

Everything you think you know and everything you actually know resides here. A conscious Universe is forever in a state of anticipation, waiting to fulfill your desires, wishes, and wants.

You may wonder, how can this be? As a human collective, you may be thinking:

Listen, Universe, I know who I am; I know my place in the world. I have a role, I have a name, and I have experiences to prove I exist in a limited world.

This limited world is something cruel. It dishes out suffering. It spits out demands. It is a trap from which there is no escape except perhaps death. Or perhaps the escape from the trap is through my belief in someone who will rescue me. Or maybe I am just a speck of nothing blowing in the wind—of no consequence to anyone, never mind this world.

Therefore, I'll play it safe by doing what I have to do to appease this fickle, unjust fate. I play a role. Or I lash out in anger. I run to something or someone I can believe in and immerse myself in. Or I run away from it all.

I might try to stay alert, waiting for the next fall. Or I escape into my habits: a drug or an elixir or a puff of smoke helps me escape, if only for a little while.

And what does a conscious and friendly Universe have to say to all of this running and reacting and withdrawal and fear and appeasement? If a conscious Universe could smile—and It can—It would smile compassionately, quietly, with no malice or judgment, and It would say:

I love you. There is nothing you need do to be a part of me except to be a part of me.

There is nothing you need do to be my beloved except to be my beloved.

So breathe and know this: All of this is Consciousness. You live in a world which shapes itself around you.

Affirming this love, we will now introduce you to the entourage which makes up a conscious Universe, for whether you are aware of this or not, all of these "players" are constantly at play in your life and the life of every form in the Universe—every single one. Wouldn't it be inspiring to know who you are playing with?

The next four chapters will introduce you to the world of Consciousness. Though it is not a new way for the Universe to play, it may be a new perspective for most of you, with new terminology to introduce the players. So we thought a brief primer would be useful. Read, study and enjoy. No need to get bogged down by any of the newer concepts. Instead, we welcome you to enjoy the ride by skipping ahead to the other downloads, if you wish.

We have waited an eternity to bring these downloads to you, so we are very, very patient—we have plenty of time.

And we welcome you to YOUR conscious Universe:

Consciousness Is the Basis of the Universe

Consciousness is the basis of the Universe and the umbrella, the container, and the all-in-all. You cannot go to where there is no Consciousness—even in destruction there is Consciousness, and even in nothingness there is Consciousness. It is all-inclusive and non-exclusive. It is the basis of all matter and non-matter. The very energy found all over the Universe is Consciousness.

The Four Forces of Consciousness

Within Consciousness, there are four players in constant play, otherwise known as the Four Forces of Consciousness: Love, Creation, Destruction, and Essence.

The Love Force is responsible for the original spark of life. Like the spark that was the Big Bang, Love began it all and then sustains it all. In the beginning was the light that was and is Love. The light of Love illuminated the Nothing (no-thing) and created thought, and then sustained the thought long enough for another force of Consciousness to take over: Creation.

Creation brings into manifestation that which was un-manifest. From Love, all creations are born, and Creation is the mechanism, the force which makes it (any of it) so. There was a character in your media, a starship Captain Picard, who would tell his first mate to "make it so."

Such is the nature of the force of Creation: Its only function is to make it so and so and so; to create, create, create.

Love then maintains a creation until the creation's term, or potential, has expired. It is then that the force of Destruction holds forth, terminating that which is to be terminated and dissolved back into Consciousness again.

At the heart of it all, if we may use the heart for diagrammatic assistance, is Essence. Essence is essential to all creation; every creation is created in order to fulfill a purpose. In fact, this is the closest term we have in the English language to describe this marvelous force: For every thing and every person, for every season in the grand cycle of life, there is a purpose.

These Four Forces of Consciousness are always in force, in simultaneous automatic play without end. You cannot have one force of Consciousness without the other three as constant companions. They interact and interweave in a beautiful dance—the dance of a conscious Universe.

Herewith are lessons in how they each play, full out. We bless your journey with them …

As a force of Consciousness, Love exists in a state of forever.

Chapter 4

The Love Force

What is Love? People on this wonderful planet see love as a tender affection or as an addiction, or as something to be longed for. Yet Love is also a dominant force in this Universe, and prevalent anywhere you might look.

As a force of Consciousness, Love exists in a state of forever. We speak not of the categories humanity has placed love into—as if love could be cordoned off. Rather, we speak of the force of Love which is all acceptance, all allowance, in all ways. For without Love, nothing—absolutely nothing—would exist. You would not exist. These words would not exist, neither would this world exist. Whether we speak of the parts of the world where darkness descends or the parts of the world that are lit up; whether we speak of the conscious awareness of people who are waking up to their true glorious selves or the vast sleepy ones who blanket the earth, all are enveloped by Love's embrace.

Love is the ultimate in allowance. It was the Love Force which brought to humanity the gift of free will. On this free-will planet, there is an allowance of all sorts of plays, dramas, comedies, and activities to take place. Here is what was created: Once Earth was formed from the nothing, it was then *in*formed by many, many different sources of influence from all over the Universe. And then Earth was gifted this ultimate freedom: Your planet was left alone to its own devices, so to speak; and so have humans been left to your own devices.

Humans were formed out of Love and then allowed the free reign to go anywhere you wished to go as part of your conscious evolution. Free will was given and received by humans as a gift—although at times you see this as a curse. Yet this is, indeed, the will of Consciousness as Creator: Humans have the opportunity to be creators as well. In essence, you as creators are allowed to destroy, to create, to love, to unite, to break apart—all is allowed on this planet. Can you see this? It is the force of Love which allows this gift.

Love stayed the hand of other universal influences that wished for a more controlled approach to an evolving planet. Love was the One who said "No. Let them evolve on their own. Let's see what happens here. Let's see if they return to the Lap of God on their own volition." And what exactly is that Lap of God? It is the Lap of Creation, where all sparks of life come into manifest form. It is rather a daunting task to explain this concept to humanity at this time—although humanity has tried to in its many religious and spiritual traditions. Let's suffice it to say that the Lap of God was also created by a love for all, with no judgment whatsoever for any of it.

For instance, in Love's eyes, evil is viewed as a valid energy on this planet of choice. Evil exists because it was allowed to express, yet there is no overall judgment of this particular malevolent, destructive energy. Rather, as in the biblical tale of the prodigal son, Love welcomes all energies—including evil—to express and then return home to the Lap of God.

Yet, because of the hue and cry of the human spirit, there will be a shift of focus on the planet. The human spirit has tired of the free-wheeling expression of the more malevolent energies as they mingle with the more benevolent energies. And so, humanity has asked for a reprieve, if you will, a reprieve you are creating as we speak. As you move towards your great awakening in the twenty-first century of your modern calendar, you will see that the ceasing of a certain perception of life will be upon you. The perceptual shift will not happen all at once; it will happen gradually, over time. But what *will* happen is that well-being and love will take predominance over the more destructive energies of anger, spite, evil, and fear.

This is not to sound overly optimistic to you. This is not to sound like so much idealistic fluff. This is a statement of fact. People are tired, and have been tired of the energies of hatred and disappointment and anger for so long that you've constructed a date to be a marker of how ready humanity is *not* to entertain drama anymore. As in the African-American spiritual song of years past, you, as humanity, "ain't gonna study war no more."

Yet, there will still be warriors. There will still be tribal lands where there will be skirmishes. There will still be strife, and there will still be people who wish to destroy.

For now, however, and forever, there is the force of Love, ever, ever flowing through the veins of humanity and through the veins of this world. We call this Love, *The Great Allowance*. Love brings all creations into forms that are sustained for more than an instant. And it is Love that allows those forms to come and to go as they will. On this planet, many forms have come and gone, come and gone. Human life-forms have been here for a long time, but actually only a brief blip of time as far as the earth's form is concerned, and definitely as far as the Universal form is concerned.

Love allows for any life-form to have a life! This is in Love's character: the allowing of all to exist in a life span of some kind. So a bee has a life span of however many months a bee has a life span, and a human has a life span of how many months, days, years, decades he or she has a life span. The life span of a mountain or the life span of a flame on a candle is incumbent upon the force of Love. Love can create and destroy all at the same time. Love is the ultimate in allowance.

With love, we ask you now: Is there any particular question you have about the force of Love?

With the force of Love, we've created a planet of such strife. At our present levels of consciousness, how can we more consciously create what it is we actually seek?

Consciousness is the watchword of this discussion, is it not? Since we are talking about Love as a force of Consciousness, your awareness of the nature of Love will bring you to an acceptance of its allowance. And knowing that Love does indeed exist along with the forces of Creation, Destruction, Essence, you will be more conscious of what you are pouring your Love into. For what you fill with your attention and intention will indeed be created. All that is created and kept alive through the Love Force running through you will be sustained. Do you understand? And so whatever you sustain with Love, or with allowance, will be maintained for as long as it is given attention.

Love is so allowing it even allows attachment to forms and ideas. Love allows attachment to ideals; it even allows attachment to Destruction. It allows *all*, as we've said. And yet as humans evolve, they grow less and less attached to any object or focus of Love. Rather, they allow the force of Love to flow through their systems.

So why have we made such a muck of it—of expressing Love in very painful ways?

Why express yourselves in painful and limited ways? That is a grand question, and unfortunate to your human mind, we are going to answer it thusly: Love accepts all. It even accepts the mind, the ego, the personality, the duality, the polarity, and every disparity you can imagine. It accepts all.

So why have you made a muck of it? Well, let's answer via the theory that you are cloistered from the influence of the rest of the Universe. Therefore the inhabitants of earth are allowed to play out your determination to wander far from the Lap of the Great Creator, otherwise known to you as God. So the muck of which you speak is the muck of attachment to acting alone and being lost—both allowed by Love. Although, please notice the burgeoning number of people who are exhausted with being alone and lost and are no longer being served by such an attachment. It is here you will see the greatest turning humanity has ever seen. This will be the turning of your attention to Love as a benevolent force.

If people were to see how loving and gracious this allowance from Creator is, then you would also express a graciousness and allowance of other life-forms, of other ways of being, of other views of Creator, of other ways of worshipping whatever entities you wish to worship, whether it's money or a god or nature or what have you. Having compassion for all these differing expressions is the way to grow more conscious and aware of Love's benevolence.

Who allowed Love to come into the planet and be such an overabundant force? The "who" is nameless, but it is a Great Creator of all creations. From those creations came more creations—and more creations from those again. Love then allowed all creations to have a time span.

Dear people, have you noticed how time is collapsing in and of itself—growing shorter and shorter in your perception? We bring this to your attention because a time draws near when Love will prevail as a dominant *form* on the planet. We are not speaking of the form of a valentine or other human-made nicety. We are saying that Love will once again be a predominant ruling energy and that Love will allow life-forms which are more life-giving, more life-acknowledging, more in the spirit of wellness and well-being to prevail. And who are these life-forms? They are humans of course, for humans have come to this great place of choice to honor their contracts with Love, with the Universe, with the planet, and with themselves.

Today, be aware of your place in the Universe and that you have a marked place. You chose to come here out of your love for the planet, out of your love for humanity. This is what humanity is struggling to take hold of: the idea that Love allows all, every single person and every single person's actions, no matter how heinous or immoral they may seem to other people. The great allowance allows all. And the time is upon you when well-being will insert its siren call into the allowance of Love, singing, "Wouldn't self-love work quite well right now?"

The great master Jeshua ben-Joseph (Jesus) spoke of such love when he admonished the people to love their neighbors as themselves. Now, we ask you, if there was no self to love, how could you then love your neighbor as you would yourself? You must start with yourself—your bright, shiny, embattled, bruised, dark and light, human and spirit, emotional and ego-focused self. Love that self impeccably, without any limits or conditions.

Love that self, and see what turns in your own particular life, and then see what turns in the lives of others again and again and again. For the force of Love is wishing to move now. Love is wishing to move through people with compassion, with care, with the knowledge that all will turn out to be well—all of it. Love wishes to express to all of its creations, "Welcome my children; welcome back home to the Lap of God."

And that is all for now.

You … create all the time, all the time, all the time— whether you know this or not, whether you are aware or not.

Chapter 5

Creation

To the human mind, Creation is one of the most misunderstood of the Four Forces of Consciousness, for Creation is seen as the province of only a few people or of a Creation entity, such as God, or of the creator gods.

Yet, Creation is available to all, for the use of all, including the animal kingdom, including the kingdom of the cells and atoms, including humanity, of course, and including any and all unformed energies in the realm of spirit.

As one of the Four Forces of Consciousness, Creation is always in play. Here's how it works: Out of the *nothing* comes a *something*. Out of the unknown arises an awareness, and then something is known, and that is a creation as well. You and everyone else create all the time, all the time, all the time—whether you know this or not, whether you are aware of your creative power or not.

From the infinite Love of Consciousness (or Source), a special opportunity for humanity is now upon you: You have the opportunity to understand you are creators as well as destroyers. You have seen yourselves as quite limited beings: limited to putting out fires, limited to facing constant drama and the forces of unbalanced destruction. It is as if humans have focused on destruction and the defense against destruction as your primary sources of creativity, and of course, that is not so.

But let us tarry in this realm and on this notion for a bit: The focus of humanity is on destruction and defense against destruction. This plays out in your everyday life: Do you not have the feeling you are just stemming the tide of destruction, whether it is the destruction of your ecosystem, the destruction of your way of life, the destruction of the cells and organs in your body little by little as you age? Are you not in a fairly constant attitude of stemming, of delaying, of defending against the forces of destruction? Can you see how this has held sway for so long that you have become habituated to this energy?

Your dawning awareness is of your actual creative power. Another way to state this is you are becoming aware that you manifest, you bring into form, you create out of nothing! Let us hold for a moment that this is truth. If so, your power of creation is not prejudiced towards any particular creation. You create what you create, based on the attention you bring to the creation. Attention is key to what you create, for what you draw your attention to will eventually be created in one form or another.

If humanity stays in the groove of focusing on putting out fires or defending against destruction, always, always preparing for the next fall, then so, too, will humanity continue to create a comprehensively defensive system of living in the world. And in this defensive system, the overwhelming creation is of walls, containers, safety, and the known. Stepping out from the known might bring you many creative solutions to your most resistant issues. Yet the solutions stay hidden in humanity's consciousness because of this persistence of paying attention to the drama of unbalanced destruction and to the stemming of that drama.

So that's what we get?

Yes. You get further drama.

Which to our minds justifies the defenses?

Absolutely. The persistence of unbalanced destruction—and the defense against destruction—is a creation! We wish to emphasize this in a more direct way: Creation happens. You are creating, whether you are aware of what is being created or have no idea of what you are up to! Creation happens, regardless of a person's attention and intention.

Now, we are not saying that you are just creating willy-nilly, at random. What we are saying is that Creation is a major force of universal Consciousness. As such, Creation is ongoing, no matter what. It happens.

Your creations, however, have a consistent order to them as you evolve out of the darkness of forgetting who you actually are. And so the Enlightenment, the grand awakening of humanity, is all about waking up to your true essence and role. And that essence and role is that of being creators in your own lives. Your allowing divinity to pour through your creations will do more to resolve all your current problems than any amount of defending against your dramas and falls. This allowance will bring a focus on enrichment and well-being to your creations.

In other words, understanding that you are creators and that you create your own dramas, your own falls, will bring to you the *concurrent resolutions* to the dramas, as well as the creation of a new way of being on the planet. We understand how this may sound like so much spiritual hubris, so much metaphysical fluff—big words with no substance behind them. Yet, the substance of the Universe being Consciousness, after all, we say that the truth is you know this at the heart of you: You are creators, though there is a huge fear of this truth. If your creative powers are true, then you will hold yourselves accountable for your creations!

You might feel it is better to stay in a state of denial of your creative powers and be in constant defense of what you fear the most.

We ourselves are always amazed at what you come up with in your use of free will. But we do find it sad that humanity consistently propels itself along the lines of defense and drama. So, in order to turn this—what is the force of Creation, and how does it operate? Isn't this what you wish to know?

Yes! Of course we do!

Creation is a dynamic force—it has movement to it. It is moving through a conscious universe.

Also:
Creation occupies space, for it *creates* space. It also creates the contents within that space.

And:
Creation occupies time, for it is the force which created time in the first place—whether it is divine time, cyclical time, or the linear time you all believe you are operating under.

So:
Creation moves and operates in time and space, for that is what the force of Creation is meant to do. It is a doing force. It brings into being; that is what it does.

Creation brings into being every *thing*. Everything and every thought-form is birthed via Creation's forces, including this planet and all its inhabitants, from the kingdoms of the seas, the rocks, the animals, the plant materials. All creations here on this special planet were birthed as an initial seed-thought-form, or seed-creation.

Creation's first step—if you look at Creation as a force that has movement, space, and time as its dimensions—is a thought is born. A thought occurs. (This is the closest we can come, using your language, to describe this initial step though there are actually no steps involved since Creation is occurring all the time. However, we wish to bring it into human terms so that you understand where it is your creations are going and just exactly how the mechanism of creating occurs.)

The thought then has a life span of some kind. It could be momentary. It could be a thought that continues to blossom and flow into more thoughts. So thoughts are manifested constantly, and what are they manifested from? Nothing. They just are. Yet the thoughts themselves are possible seeds for creations.

There have been great wisdom teachers who stated, "Thoughts are actually things; your thoughts create your life." And yet there has also been great confusion about this for you might notice that not every single thought you have is created, right? Not all of your thoughts come into creation.

Thank goodness!

It would be quite a different world if this were so. However, some of the more stable thought-forms do persist and come into creation, and that is the key. After thought-forms are born, the more persistent thoughts are what are eventually created. Creation takes a thought. Creation takes persistence of those thoughts, and then Creation takes action of some kind, bringing the thought-forms into a manifested form of some kind.

In order to come into being, the creation thought needs to land somewhere—it needs to be perceived and received in order to be created. So, where do these thoughts land, and by whom are these thought-forms received? And the answer is: All thought-forms are received by all the entities who also contribute their thought-forms to the whole of creation.

Some of the more persistent thought-forms on the planet have come and gone, come and gone—only to arise in your consciousness again, to be created again. One of the more persistent thought-forms is that you are limited in your creative powers. Then you break out of those limitations briefly, only to be bombarded with mass consciousness thought-forms that yes, indeed, you are quite, quite limited.

Another thought-form which has held sway within humanity is the thought-form creation of slavery; an enslavement to someone or something. It's interesting how slave consciousness has held sway for many, many eons in human consciousness! Why is this? Why has slavery consistently been created? Because of the predominant thought-form of limitation. If you are a limited creator, and you are focusing on your limitations, then you will be constantly seeking outside of yourself that which will enable you to create your sustenance and your world.

This persistent looking outside of oneself in order to find the source of your sustenance keeps the enslavement energy alive. For eons, one culture or another has been either the slave keepers, or the enslaved. There is not one culture that has not been in either of those two created roles.

What we are suggesting to you is that slavery is rampant in this world as an unconscious creation. We gently say to you that you are bringing much energy to this enslavement creation—and so you find yourself enslaved to all manner of creations! For instance, you're enslaved to a monetary system that does not work well for the great majority of humanity. You're enslaved to your thoughts of defending against possible destruction. You are enslaved to a war mentality rather than a mentality of well-being.

So, too, are you enslaved by your habits and addictions—until the time you wake up to the fact that these habits and addictions no longer serve you. It is then another creation has a possibility of occurring: the evolution from slave consciousness into a consciousness of freedom.

On an individual basis, this is not easy to enact, and we understand this. It is far easier to see yourself as enslaved and trapped within your enslaved thoughts of defense against destruction and of seeking the source of power from outside yourself. It is far easier to succumb to those pernicious thought-forms. A bit more difficult is to entrust your lives to thought-forms of creativity, well-being (both personal and group well-being), kindness, compassion, understanding, and even if you do not fully understand this, the path toward solutions.

We now speak to each of you as an individual human being: When you as a soul decided to make your entrance into the world, you held such high regard for yourself! You knew you were a spiritual entity, creating and contributing to the whole in a most powerful way. And so you thought to yourself, why not bring your contribution to this beautiful planet of choice? Why not bring your creative power to this planet and assist in the resolution of the planet's more persistent, darker creations? Why not indeed?

And so, by your choice, you came to the planet with high ideals held in your heart and soul, raring to go! Then, you arrived into a world of judgment, defense against the unknown, prejudices, pain, suffering, light chased by the darkness, disease and un-ease, and so forth. In other words, you arrived in a world of duality—a division in your attention.

Perhaps your soul arrived within the body of a person born to a mother who loved and nurtured you. Perhaps you arrived in a body to a mother who abandoned you. Perhaps you arrived in the body of a person in a culture that is at war with another culture. Perhaps you arrived in the body of a person who has been offered everything in life. Perhaps you arrived in a body of a person with very little offered. Regardless of what body you've arrived in, you might admit to yourself that the high ideals held by your soul as it transferred to a body were rather lost in translation, creating a whole different story.

You arrived as an enthusiastic soul with ideals who had "squeezed" yourself into a very limited creation. The execution of your ideals lost a lot in the squeezing. Yet, we suggest that this is the prime challenge to choosing a life on this planet: What will you do, even with these limitations? And what will you create with these limited thoughts? What can be created out of your addiction to destruction and defense? What can be created out of your focus on well-being? What a magnificent challenge! It is absolutely brilliant what humanity has created here, even though some of you see it as absolutely stupid what you have created here. There is brilliance in all of this creation of destruction and defense and division and judgments. Of all the opportunities you've had to create, you created this world—and we are astonished.

Now, however, there is the sense that humanity tires of this particular creation. What has to change in order for you to create something different? None other than your thoughts, so that what you create with those thoughts will change as well. This sounds all so simple, does it not? And in essence, it is simple. Yet we also admit that the complexity comes after the original seed-thought occurs. Your attention to the thought-form and the persistence of the thought-form is what you eventually manage to create. To review: Creation takes a thought, it takes attention to the thought, it takes persistence of the thought, and then an action of some kind. This can be an action on your part, an action on another person's part, an action of a whole group, an action from an animal, an action from an entity, an action of some kind—something happens, and there is creation.

So let's back up a bit—back to an original thought. If the thought is temporary and has no attention paid it, it will not persist, and it will not be created in form. So do not worry too much about some of your more negative thought-forms. If they come up, and you are aware of them, you might bring to your mind something different—perhaps focusing on what it is you intend to create. The stronger thought-forms—those with more attention paid to them—will indeed be created. Do you understand how this goes?

In your current situation, we wish to applaud you, for you have been playing at the edges of creation and destruction for many years of your time together here, if not your entire lifetimes. You have seen some of your creations go by the wayside in your mind and perception, for you have thought, "Oh, this is only temporary. This cannot persist." Thus your fears and defenses against the fears have actually created the destruction of some of your greater dreams. Now however, we are seeing a shift in you all, and so we offer our encouragement: Keep your focus and your attention on your desired creations. You are creating magnificent creations that will bring feelings of well-being to many, many people. Through these creations you will prosper, for the universe supports *all* of your creations—whatever you pour your attention into.

May we further suggest: Pour your attention into thoughts of well-being, of justice, of honor, of compassion, and of course, of healing. Consistently hold these thoughts in front of you, even if the world temporarily looks as if it is not supporting these thoughts. Every single day of your lives, you get hints from the universe as to what you are creating, how it is you are creating, and how to bring your ideals to life. And by ideals, we speak of your soul's ideals. Remember the soul who came to earth in order to manifest such high ideals? There is nothing wrong with ideals. Ideals are not to be bashed. Ideals need to be in existence in order for humanity to evolve, since ideals provide something to evolve towards.

OK, creators: What is it you wish to focus on? Which thoughts do you want to bring into creation? What is the greater purpose of these thought-forms coming into creation? What dramas are you supporting with your thought-forms? What fears are you supporting with your thought-forms? What answers are you supporting with your thought-forms? What creations are you creating with your thought-forms? These are all questions that you are growing in awareness of. We say this with the utmost sincerity: Having in mind these creation questions will enable a great shift in human consciousness and creation.

The time of shifting your persistent creations into creations you actually desire as a soul group is upon you. As well, though, the persistent creations of enslavement, destruction, and defense of drama will have their say! So you need to acknowledge this: There is a battle going on—a grand battle—with all who take part in it the eventual winner.

If destructive thoughts can be held in compassion, then you will see the forces of creativity and aliveness come into play. Look through the eyes of a compassionate creator, for this is who you are. Look through the eyes of an idealistic creator, for this is who you are as well. We have heard the cry of the souls who wish to create a world of balance and beauty, and this is why we are saying to you how we hold you dear as fellow creators of a most abundant universe.

That is all for now.

You are the children of Consciousness, after all, so you are all growing up and learning that which you already know.

Chapter 6

The Essence

Infused into all life-forms is a template, an instructional vibration, that can be termed Essence. It is the full potential of each and every creation, from micro to macro creation; from subatomic to stellar. All possibilities are within the Essence. The essential nature of each creation puts out a signature message that is interpreted through the perception of all other creations. Therefore life, all of life, is a perception.

Essence provides this crucial information: For what purpose is a creation created? And the answer to that question is as infinitely varied as the infinite variety of creations. All that is created in form has a purpose and is part of the magnificent balancing act that is this known and still unknown universe.

All the steps to a creation's full potential are included in the Essence. Within the confines of the planet, Essence is the balancing force of everything here since it ascribes a purpose to each creation. Essence as the balancer is also the potentiator, allowing for something to express itself to its greatest potential—in the fullness of itself.

Human essence is rich and complex and wildly varied. And yet, held within human essence is the potential to not reach his or her potential or partially reach it or fully reach it. Recall how there is a term, "fully realized," in the truth teachings of certain spiritual masters? What does this term actually mean? To state this as simply as humanly possible, full realization of each human equals self-realization. It is knowing you are Consciousness incarnate. And within this realization there are no limits to what a human can create or destroy or love. You are the children of Consciousness after all, and you are all growing up and learning that which you already know.

Which brings us back to Essence: Essence is that which you already know. Essence is that which anything or anyone already knows. In order to determine the essence of anything, ask this simple question: "What do you know?" For instance, "Lion, what do you know?" And it might answer: "I know how to meet my daily food. I know the power of tribal cooperation."

Or you might ask, "River rock, what do you know?" And the rock might answer, "I know how to tumble in the stream. I use adversity to shape me into a thing of beauty. I go with the flow of life, yet I know how to settle for a time."

And you might ask yourself the same question. Who knows what the answer might be?

All creations have an essence. It is incumbent on you, a fellow creation, to acknowledge this essence. To acknowledge the essence is to shine a light on the knowledge contained within the creation.

Remember, Consciousness is and always will be.

However:

Being conscious of Consciousness is an option.

Being conscious of your essence is an option.

Having the option to be conscious or not is made possible through the force of Love.

Remembering who you are, forgetting who you are ... Consciousness requires nothing from you, so you live within the vast in-between of forgetfulness and remembrance. While you are here, you might as well play with the forces of Consciousness. Isn't that what Consciousness as the parent of us all would want?

Go. Play. Discover your true essence. Enjoy your potential. And love what you know.

That is all for now.

You are the children of Consciousness, after all, so you are all growing up and learning that which you already know.

Chapter 7

A Time for Everything, Including Destruction

We continue our discussion of how the Four Forces of Consciousness are in operation constantly, forever, and we do mean forever. There is no beginning or end to these forces. The Four Forces of Consciousness are at play in your everyday lives and in the life span of every creation in the Universe. And the universe you know of and most certainly the Universe you do not know of *exists* because Consciousness is the basis of that Universe.

Let's reintroduce the Four Forces of Consciousness: Creation brings into form. Destruction destroys a form. Love sustains a form. And then there is a fourth force which is rather an enigma—if Consciousness itself is not enigma enough for those of you studying it—Essence. Some synonyms for Essence would be source, seed, core value, and the best synonym: *purpose.*

Time as a Convenience

Digressing to essence/purpose for a moment—there is an eloquent passage in one of your holy books, the Bible, "To everything there is a season, and a time to every purpose under heaven." What this suggests is for every purpose, for every essence, there is a season, and every season has its purpose in the great balancing act that is Consciousness at play. There is a season and a cycle for every creation in the Universe.

Time is a field on which the Four Forces of Consciousness play. Time is a convenience, much as an athletic field is a convenience for the play or a soccer pitch is a convenience for the play or an open field is a convenience for a child to play, pick flowers, and watch clouds. So time is a convenience as it is a field for awareness. Without time, there would be no awareness of separate creations in the process of having a life-span because everything would be happening at once. The truth is, everything IS happening at once in the greater Consciousness—as we say, the Four Forces of Consciousness are simultaneously at play with every form in the universe. So time is a convenience for you and other living forms, allowing you to perceive seasons, separation, and even your individuality.

For convenience sake, let's perceive each life-form as having a cycle. In the beginning of a cycle, there is no *thing* … nothing. Everything is created out of this nothing—it is pure potential.

And then something happens! A creation occurs. A creation, such as a cat purring in a morning beam of sunshine, has an intimate relationship with the world from the very instant it is created in form—from a single cell to a kitten to the full grown cat purring in the sunshine. The cat has a form, and then that form has a life span.

Picture this life span carving out a circle. After a while, the cat's form starts breaking down as part of her life cycle. She moves slower in her old age, and different systems are starting to be destroyed, breaking down. But even for the cat to exist in a healthy form, systems within her had to break down and be destroyed. During her life cycle, cells came and went, billions of them. She breathed in an uncountable number of atoms and molecules, which have circulated through her small form.

In order for the cat to remain a cat, some things had to be destroyed—otherwise the cat would not be a healthy cat for very long. Do you understand us so far? She would start out as a healthy cat and then turn into something else such as a cat with cancer, since cancer cells are formed and then grow without any interruption in their growth.

Back to this cat: Systems are breaking down and eventually the form of a cat will cease to exist—no more will she be this cat. The circle is complete for this creation. There may be some fur and bones left, yet after a while, that will change as well and become rock or oil or dust—different creations which will have a cycle all their own, eventually returning to the great nothing.

And this is just one cat. There's an entire universe in a cat, and she is playing her part in the creation of it. This happens with every single creation. Every creation is created, exists for a span of time, and finally disintegrates into nothing; or to put it into Consciousness terms: Every creation eventually returns to pure potential. There is no creation in the universe that is forever, with one great exception: Consciousness is in a state of forever.

The mystery is: How was Consciousness created? That will always be a mystery to your mind. There can be transcendental experiences which point to this. For instance, near death experiences often include a feeling of infinity and an expansion into that infinity. Also within those transcendent experiences, there may be a review of an individual's purpose in life—a reminder to you that there are reasons and seasons and purposes for every single form in the universe. How are those purposes determined—assigned, if you will? Again, this will be a mystery. But suffice it to say that Creation happens, Destruction also happens, and in the meantime, the other two essential forces of Consciousness are at play: Love and Essence. When something is created, it is created with an essence/purpose. For instance, the essential nature of a cat is there and is not the same essential nature as, say, a bird. Or a chair. Or a tree. There is an essential nature to a poem, and there's an essential nature to you. There is an essence of you. And that essence guides your purpose for being as it guides the purpose for the cat's being.

Meanwhile, there is another force at play, a grand force all over the universe, and that is the force of Love. Love is connection. Love creates the relationships of everything to everything else. Love forms the basis of the relationship of the moon to the earth or of one particle to another. Even a human attracted to another human in any way, shape, or form has the force of Love at play, no matter how that attraction occurs. Even an attraction to another human via what you call hate has the underlying force of Love at play if you were but to look at the relationship through the lens which views a greater picture.

For every human, there is a relationship to all the other humans on the planet, to the planet itself, to Consciousness of course, to everything. Love has been the force which has bonded humans to each other in tribal units, in whole countries, and in large groupings and tiny groupings, one to another, small family units, mother to baby, and so on. Love is the ultimate in entanglement.

Conscious Destruction

You've become increasingly aware of the force of Destruction at play in the world. You are beginning to notice how the suppression of destruction may not be the best method deployed by humans in order to create a world of well-being. Let's explore the force of Destruction in a more healing and uplifting way, for the force of Destruction will be with you always—just as the force of Love will be, just as the force of Creation will be, just as the Essence will be forever entwined with these forces.

In the spirit of this compassionate download, you need to understand that the force of Destruction cannot be suppressed in a healthful way unless there is an awareness of the essence of Destruction. Yes, there is a reason for destruction to exist.

For instance, within the body system you cannot be who you are without destruction happening all the time, all the time. Cells are coming and going and coming and going. They are created and have a purpose and a life span and then are destroyed. There would be no person reading this download, nor would there be the person bringing through the download, without this constant expression of Consciousness. So, destruction comes in quite handy!

If a certain insect that loves to munch on tree bark exists—and there are many such animals—there is nothing inherently evil in its existence. Perhaps, as they munch on downed and dead trees, they create fertilizer for the next batch of trees, since they excrete fertilizer. However, if these same insects were to munch on a live tree, then that tree would be destroyed. Again there is nothing inherently evil in this. This interaction happens all the time, and when the tree ceases to exist, it becomes fertilizer and food for the rest of the system.

Now imagine well-meaning people who wished to destroy a certain predator in the forest because the predator was invading their crops and destroying them. Due to the elimination of the predator, which also happens to eat these insects, the insects multiply uncontrolled and, therefore, destroy an entire forest. You understand? Again, there is nothing inherently evil here. There's always a reason for any destructive force. Remember, Destruction has its own purpose and essence, of course, since all the forces are operating at the same time. Yet when certain actions produce the consequence of unbalanced destruction, people might view the insect as the enemy.

Who Is the Enemy?

In the case of people who are seen as an enemy, they are usually viewed as an enemy because they are threatening something you love, is that not true? Enemies are made of people you perceive as wanting to destroy what you have a connection to, a relationship with—whether it is your family, your country, another loved one, or even a complete stranger. If you see someone who has just committed an assault on another someone, and even if those two are complete strangers, would you not be moved by this? There is someone who is perceived as an enemy of some kind, an evil assaulting an innocent. And this experience reinforces the notion that enemies and evil are everywhere.

Enemies are constantly being created by your perception. Evil is a creation of convenience, human-constructed within your minds so that you might explain why destruction has gone out of control within the human story.

When one is fighting a perceived enemy, you need to know that this perceived enemy is perceiving you as an enemy as well because he or she also has Love, Destruction, Creation, and Essence at work within his or her system. There could be many different reasons for proclaiming him or her an enemy of yours. Perhaps both of you have a love of a country or a god or a culture, and each of you sees the other as threat to this love—and so the battle begins.

In the Balance

What human consciousness is trying to grasp are the following questions: Where is the balance of these eternal forces? How can you support the balance so that well-being is supported on planet Earth? In these times of increasing awareness—and, as well, increasing challenges—understanding the role of the Destruction Force is essential in considering the balance of all the other forces at play.

Indeed, you have created complex relationships here. We absolutely honor this. And it is fascinating how obsessed you have become with the forces of Destruction. We acknowledge there is nothing inherently evil in this. Yet understand that your focusing on the force of Destruction without the concurrent realization of other forces in play will bring you further destruction of what you do not wish to destroy.

An awareness of the balance of your human interaction with the Four Forces might be welcome. Each one of you can work with the balance thusly: First of all, have an understanding of the essence of different cultures—what people love and cherish and have relationship with is essential to them. Otherwise, when you perceive people as a stated enemy, you will have no idea who you are actually battling. Therefore battles will continue and fester and grow and continue some more, for there is no particular purpose to the battle except to destroy those who are perceived as enemy.

On an individual and group level, do your best to discover and relate to the essence and purpose of your fellow humans. Explore how they view their relationship to their country or tribe or religious belief or cultural roles and so on.

Secondly, ask: What is in the balance here? What are the consequences to your actions? If you do battle, what will you create, and what will you destroy? As you ask this, you will not necessarily receive simple answers, of course. You might receive complex answers, but at least you will understand a little more about what you are about to do and what consequences might come from those actions.

Lastly, the force of Love can never be underestimated. It is always at work in the human form, since the force of Love sustains all created forms. In considering any actions with any other human, one needs to take into consideration what the other one is in relationship with. How strong is that relationship to a body, to a village, to a country, to a belief, to a system, to a god … to anything? Out of these relationships, attachments are often made. And it is those attachments that need to be carefully considered and compassionately worked with.

By the way, consider this: There is never just one person at play, in isolation, in any given war situation. For instance, Hitler did not operate in isolation to create a war—of course not. If he was just a maniac operating in isolation, he would have killed perhaps a few people, not millions. But he had a relationship to others and their attachment to a way of life. In other words, there was the force of Love at work. See how powerful Love can be? If Consciousness is the basis of the Universe, no one acts in isolation. Even a hermit is not in isolation for there is always a relationship to something.

As to decrying one person as an enemy who needs to be destroyed at all costs—well, there is something about that person who engages other people to support his or her view, right? So, the relationships are there. Why? That is what you need to discover. Why do people hold certain ideas in great esteem over other ideas? In other words what is the essence of the idea? What is their purpose for being? When ideas are formed, they either die a quick death in the human mind, or they are supported somehow.

Try to understand why these particular ideas are supported and upheld and brought into forms, such as cultural rules, beliefs, opinions, or agendas. Work on these aspects of your conflicts—the purpose of the conflict; why it was created in the first place; who is that enemy and what is that person supporting—and you will have an easier time as you untangle the knots upholding the creation of war and unbalanced destruction.

And that is all for now.

Any person can decide that fear is unnecessary—even in the face of fearful circumstances.

Chapter 8

Through the Eyes of Fear

*W*ell *spirit, I'm looking at the world through the eyes of fear—fearing my personal future. I feel as if I am at war with myself, wondering whether I'm good enough or up to the task of bringing through this important information. So, today I would like to address fear.*

I know people are in intense fear this very second—there are many people somewhere being threatened or hurt, or who are sick or facing death or pain or loss. So fear of any of the above is always with us, it seems. I also would like to understand the kind of fear that is persistent, low-grade, always in the background, never far from our thoughts.

How do we collectively and individually keep fear going? And why do we do that? What is fear, and what can be done about it?

Fear was originally created as a device to keep a physical entity safe from destructive forces so that an entity could survive another moment or another day and live out its particular life for however long that life would be. For instance, in the case of an animal such as a deer, fear is merely the device that helps the deer put into motion the "fight or flight" hormones and chemistry and muscle action so that it might flee a predator if it is meant to flee.

Fear was originally a physical safety and balance device, including for human beings, so that there would be a balance of standing at a cliff's edge yet not going any further. When one is in a situation somewhat tenuous to the body, fear would arise in the body just enough for the body to react and remove itself from the source of the fear.

Fear was not developed as a way to torture an entity or bring that entity to its knees in more fear. Again, its original purpose was to keep an entity safe from physical harm. Fear is healthy in minute doses if it is there to nudge one to act or react for the safeguarding of the entity's body vehicle.

Now, however, the habitual pattern of fear is entrenched within the human form, which renders fear as just another emotion. Fear creates all kinds of havoc in a system when it is there all the time—when it is lurking, as you put it.

Fear is at the heart of so many illnesses, so many destructive actions, and so many mental illnesses. It feeds all manner of systems you have put into place, including religious systems, economic systems, governance, treatment of the genders, the races, of children versus adults, how you treat your illnesses, how you approach problems, and so forth. Many of these systems are based on a less-than-appropriate use of the device called "fear."

And so, the low-grade fear you feel is persistent within humanity's operating system, to use the analogous computer terminology. So much so, no one even questions it.

People are quite addicted to fear. You are addicted to fear's chemical reaction and addicted to the reaction in the body. You might ask yourselves: If you are not in some kind of fear state, with its concurrent reaction/action, then are you truly alive?

Conversely, could you actually be at peace, 24/7? Is that possible, and still feel aliveness in a body and in life? These questions are rarely, if ever, asked in any given lifetime or within humanity's construction of reality.

Yet in a few traditions of spirit, including Buddhism, there is acknowledgement of the suffering fear produces—the main fear being of losing what one is attached to. With this acknowledgement, one will have compassion for suffering and, as well, simultaneously acknowledge this profound possibility: Suffering can end.

So there is some headway made toward challenging your pernicious, fear-based attitudes and beliefs. Mind you, it is not that practicing Buddhists do not feel low-grade fear. In fact, even while in meditation, people who are not in the center of themselves quite yet will have fear break through the surface of their consciousness, invading their meditations.

However, as we say, headway has been made within this one spiritual path, as well as other more individual paths: Any person can decide that fear is unnecessary—even in the face of fearful circumstances. There are people who are entirely at peace in the middle of wartime, for instance. And there are people who are at peace in the middle of a storm or in the middle of a painful illness. There are people who are at peace and not fearing death even as they face death. True enough, the peaceful ones are in the distinct minority, and yet the fact of the matter is they are here, on your planet of choice, and are choosing to be at peace in that particular moment.

Dear Elke, we address you now: When you sign off on your phone message machine, you use a phrase: "Be at peace within yourself." Why do you use that phrase?

Because it sets me at ease, and I have this feeling that it will set other people at ease as well.

True enough, and yet where did this phrase come from? Did you pick it up from a book or a tract or a spiritual teacher?

No, I just started saying it a few years ago. It was just the thing to say.

Exactly. It came from within yourself, acknowledging the peace within other selves. "Be at peace within yourself" are the watchwords for the next century. In the noise and the drama all around you, the least you can do is be at peace within yourself—and it is the best you can do as well.

To be at peace within oneself is not to deny the fear there. We are not speaking about denial in any form. To be at peace within oneself means one chooses peace in any given moment.

Peace within may be momentary; it may last a millisecond, or it may last several hours, days, or years—time is inconsequential. To choose to be at peace within oneself is to honor your greatest gift: You have never, ever lost the true Self, the true Being-ness of you—ever. Despite each human forgetting this over and over and over again, the true Self never forgets you. Your Self never forsakes you, is always available, and is always at peace.

So, to be at peace within yourself is a direct acknowledgement of this relationship of human to being.

I am watching a child playing on the sand right now—joyfully, easily. This begs the question: What can you say to the human who's been traumatized in life as a child?

I also just spent an entire weekend with people who have travelled to the "other side" in their near death experiences and have come back to the planet. Most are facing damaged bodies, brains, sometimes souls. How can I say to them that "your Self has never abandoned you"? And how can I say that to myself when there have

been times in my life when I have felt very abandoned? Frankly,
that's rather difficult for the human to accept as fact.

We have great compassion for your honesty. The honest human accepts the fact that the Self never abandons one, but as well, the honest human also accepts this: The human does abandon the Self. This is a perception, of course. But consider this:

"Being" is always available. Your Self is always present.

We say this very slowly and gently to you: Always.

Take a look at people who are in crisis—tragedy, accident, illness, crisis of faith, job loss, financial disaster, etc.—when they let go to the crisis and the ensuing chaos, that is when they often find their inner peace. Haven't you observed this in a few humans? It is when that person is in the middle of a terror that he or she can let go to his or her peace. And how is it that this can actually happen? Because it does happen. It does happen. There must be some relationship there, mustn't there be?

And so we say with great love and admiration and compassion and with no derision on our part: It is the human who often abandons the being, or the Self—and not the other way around. You abandon the Self in your limited consciousness. You abandon the Self with your thoughts as you become acculturated, as you become addicted to fear, as you become entrenched within the common perception of a world as a fearsome place, with you only a small cog in the machine or a speck of no consequence to anything or anyone.

Yet, as to this child playing in the sand, he does not see himself as a speck! Right now, he is the center of his universe. And he might as well be the center of the Universe, as he makes footprints in the sand and leaps about in joy! There are no thoughts of "How important am I here?" or "What difference am I making?" or even "Where is my next meal coming from?" At this moment, he is pure play and joy. And this is a goal for the planet we all share: that the planet's children and the child within each adult human being can experience this freedom, no matter what circumstances surround them.

The Body Vehicle

So let us address fear again.

First of all, let's acknowledge that the root of fear comes from a survival mechanism or device created solely for the purpose of keeping the body vehicle safe. Understanding this, you can then have compassion for yourself when you are in fear.

Also understand this: The body is a vehicle. It can be much like a car vehicle or a horse that you ride or any other vehicle. It can be great fun to operate or a chore to operate—your perception of this is key.

Using the example of a roller coaster—this vehicle is great fun to some and of great terror to others. And so, too, for the body-vehicle: The body will react in occasional fear—it just will. That is a natural part of its composition. So acknowledging this and acknowledging that the human, who operates in time and space within the vehicle of a body—a vehicle perceived as separate from the being—will often automatically feel fear.

But even as a child, such as the child playing on the sand, will feel fear once in a while, if it is a healthy fear and keeps one safe, he will not react in ways that will bring on an *unhealthy* fear. Rather, he will have a healthy, boundaried fear of, say, a cliff-side. And if he wishes to climb the cliff; it is then he will take the appropriate actions to keep his body vehicle safe. You understand?

A body feeling fear is a natural state of being in a world of time and space. The being—a.k.a. the Self—however, does not have any such fears or any such mechanisms to keep itself separate from the rest of the world, including the body.

So the Self never abandons the body! But the body forgets that the Self is present and always will be. When this forgetting happens often enough, feeling fear will support this perception of separation: "Oh! When I am in fear, I am alone and defenseless." Or, "I need to stay in that fear in order to protect the body."

This is when beliefs about who you are take hold, such as, "We are only bodies, operating on a material planet. We are chemical factories on legs. We are separate from the Universe." The truth is there is separation. But the truth *also* is there is always Self. There is always being.

So let's address fear in a given moment—especially when the fear persists and does not release to a friendlier Universe or release to peace within oneself. First and foremost, the fear needs to be addressed. What is at the root or the core of the fear? Is it body survival? Is it the fear of pain? Is it a fear of abandonment by others so that you will be a lone soul in the world? Is it a fear that Creator or the Universe will abandon you altogether? Could it be that you see your actions as not good enough for a Creator who might punish you if you do not obey the rules—whatever they might be?

All these fears are persistent within most humans. And so to acknowledge that a fear has been created within a human is a good first step. Simply acknowledge that the fear *is*. You don't have to do anything about it right away.

Second step: As you acknowledge that fear is present, you might notice that your breath has become short, and you are breathing in the upper regions of your lung capacity with only a bare minimum of breath being taken in and expelled.

To the human body and form, this is a signal that says, "We are not going to survive! Death is imminent! Destruction or pain is imminent!" Acknowledge the fear, and then acknowledge what kind of breath you are taking in: Is it shallow?

Next, breathe. If it is difficult for you to breathe, make the effort to breathe anyway. Do whatever it takes to take a bit of a breath, deeper and deeper into your body vehicle. This makes a simple statement to your human: You wish to live, at least for another moment. There is safety in that moment because there is being in that moment.

People attuned to martial arts acknowledge this. They have mastered the breath and have, therefore, mastered their fear. And yes, mastering fear is possible!

After all, fear is a device in the human vehicle. Therefore, much as one might master a vehicle such as a car, an airplane, or a bicycle, one can also master fear in a body. Fear is not the driver of the vehicle, even though you have made it out to be.

Acknowledge that fear is in existence and it is a device. Acknowledge that, when in fear, you are more likely to breathe quite shallowly, which allows the body to feel and react to the fear over and over again.

Then acknowledge that you are the master of the vehicle. You are the driver. Do you wish to be driving something fast and furious, slow and gentle, or something in between? The vehicle of the human body can be all these things! Even if you are a quadriplegic, you can drive the vehicle. If you have no eyes, then it is still possible to drive your vehicle.

We have been speaking mostly of the pernicious, low-grade fear which occasionally flares and brings people to seeing themselves as limited. This is the fear that has driven the systems of human interaction for so long.

When humans, one by one, community by community, start to operate from a place of a true Self who always wants what is most balancing and in the highest interest of all, then major shifts will occur in governance, in economic flow, in the distribution of services and goods, in the realm of healing and problem solving.

Whole societies based on fears will be healed by acknowledging that no true Self has ever abandoned anyone, nor have the Selves ever abandoned a group. Furthermore, the Universe has never abandoned the Earth! If you are human, though, you have abandoned your potential. You have abandoned your knowing who you are—just so you can experience separation. You can even experience fear as a device gone wild.

So we suggest that in a moment of fear, take a breath. And then another. Acknowledge there is a root cause driving the fear, and then take another breath. Understand that your true Self is there. Understand there is peace within yourself.

Feel Alive, With or Without Fear

Spirit, I wonder why it is we seek out fear. We go to movies which are fear-producing or choose to participate in dangerous activities. Fear drives our media and our very lifestyles. What keeps us attached to something we try to avoid as well?

Interestingly enough, the core of any addiction is attachment to something that one also wishes to avoid.

People become attached to fear early on in life. Within a human with a memory and a consciousness, the memory of a fearsome event can settle into the body and something is acknowledged: When a human feels fear, the human also feels very alive! Something radical is occurring in the body: Chemicals are flowing; systems are operating at full speed. So the feelings of aliveness are what keep a person addicted to fear.

When those fearful feelings wane, some people feel dulled-down, as if their life force is vacating and is not available.

We need to stress this now: There does not have to be fear in order to feel alive. When one is in a state of peace, one can also be in a state of profound aliveness. Some people have a preference for feeling occasional fear because it is seen as a variation on aliveness—yet not necessarily the only source of aliveness. It is all a matter of personal choice. Some people love to be on the roller coaster of life. They will do things which are adrenaline-charging or fearsome in their impact. These people attend and create movies, plays, and other venues which are fear-inducing. Again this is a personal choice.

The great mystery of what humanity chooses as a group or as an individual will remain a mystery. There is no particular reason for any human to feel any amount of fear for any amount of time. Fear was originally a device for maintaining the survival of the vehicle—and that is all. It was taken, though, into the mix of choices available to the humans, and the tenor of fear changed from a simple protective device to an emotional reaction. Again, there is great mystery in this: Why is it some people feel more alive in wartime and others feel much more alive in peacetime? Why is it that some people prefer peaceful soothing music and others prefer loud and raucous sounds? Why is it that some people dance and other people sit out the dance? Why do some people appreciate the fruits of fear and others prefer to be in the quietude of peace? Why is it that humans often do not choose peace? Once again, "the mystery" is needed as a way of explaining what humans do.

Peace can come in the midst of fear, of course, and the choice of being at peace within oneself is always available, no matter what is going on. That is the truth of your lives. For now, be at peace within yourself, for you are, indeed, creating from your Self as well as from your fears. If fear is overwhelming, then go to the heart of the matter, breathe into it, and bring your human self face to face with your true Self so that you may feel the unconditional, unbridled, unlimited love of your being.

Feel the Love Force flow through your life just as strong as the force of fear. You are meant to be agents of play on the planet so it does not have to be one way or another, fearful or peaceful. You can feel fear if the body deems it necessary, but you do not have to become attached to the fear. You don't even have to become attached to peace or attached to the Self because the Self will never leave you, will never go away.

And that is all for now.

Every day, you are held entranced by the spell of your beliefs—every day. To acknowledge this truth will be very freeing for you. If you know you are so entranced by your beliefs, then you have the choice to wake up from the entrancement!

Chapter 9

Power of Belief

If this is a planet of free choice, where do the gods or does a God fit in?

Well then, what is begged for is a discussion on the tool of belief.

First, we wish to state for the record that there is indeed a Creative Force in the universe. Human beings have named this force God, Allah, gods, goddesses, and the Great Goddess—the latter based on the belief in a divine Mother who birthed all life into form and who provides nurturance for her creations. And there is great truth to these beliefs. There is truth to a male aspect of a god in the form of a Father who tends to his children. And there is truth as well to a belief in ten thousand gods or five hundred thousand gods or a pantheon of gods and creator spirits familiar to the people of ancient Greece, Sumeria, Egypt, Europe, Asia, Africa, aboriginal people the world over, and so on and on …

Why? Why indeed such a variety? Why the pantheons vs. the oneness? Why the One vs. the others? Because your faith as a human being, as a materialized spirit, has been in a Creation Source of some sort. In essence, you had a fundamental faith in an attentive, conscious

Universe and a faith in Consciousness as the basis of that universe forever. It is just that Consciousness, via Love's insistence, has allowed you to believe anything you wish to believe.

Belief is a very potent tool on this planet of choice. Without belief, no human-made thing would be formed, and no human-made thing would last for more than a moment.

We have stated once before that Love creates the possibility for any one form to have a life span: a tree, an insect, a human, or a thought. Yet it is your beliefs that have set humans apart from all the other animals on this planet. Human beliefs created the planet as it is today and as it was yesterday and as it was thousands of years ago. For as long as there have been humans on the planet, there have been human beliefs at play with all Four Forces of Consciousness: Creation, Destruction, Love, and Essence.

Beliefs offer structure. They trap a thought into a habitual form enough so that the thought is sustained. What you believe is what you will actually perceive. Once a belief becomes a habit, the structure of the belief offers the human a comfort zone to reside in.

Beliefs offer context—they set up the play, whether it's going to be a drama, a comedy, an improvisational piece, or a ballet or a symphony or a drumming ceremony or what have you. Beliefs add color, dimension, structure. They set the stage, bring in the players, bring in the direction; they even bring in an occasional director or directors.

Beliefs fill out the picture. They bring in details, richness, and dynamism. For on this planet of choice, it is as if you all landed on the Planet of the Great Buffet Table! Many, many options are available to you as to how you might proceed to create your lives. It doesn't really matter wherever it is humanity actually came from or wherever any life-form came from; what does matter is the variety of life which added spice to this place. And though this may be hard for some of you to believe, at some point in your history, you chose to be left alone to your own devices.

A very long time ago, in your reckoning of time, a choice was made to be in creation every moment of your lives. All of you wished for the opportunity to choose from and create from the buffet of available choices how you were going to live out your days as materialized spirits.

You planted yourselves here for a temporary time to act out the play of forgetting who you are as spiritual beings. Why? While you were drawn into the material plane, there was also the plan to eventually journey back to "home base," if you will, back to the Lap of God. The path to Separation and the path to Unity were created simultaneously—what an adventure!

But as to your question about the creator gods vs. an overall god, and how a creator or creators affected this planet, we have this to say: Love was the force which directed a conscious Universe to put together a place where *all* would be allowed. ALL. Everything and anything would go.

Various beliefs were then formed from your experiences with this allowance—people acquired different tastes. Therefore, as you travel the planet, people have different tastes in their experiences—even in their foodstuffs, yes? So, too, you have different tastes in God. Your beliefs add spice, which enlivens each of those tastes so that, when those tastes become habituated, you create unique sacred forms. You create myths and stories. You perform rituals based on those stories and myths. You run your lives from your beliefs.

All people are trying to point back to an original Source Consciousness. Some of you point through dancing. Some of you point through singing. Some of you point through meditation. Some of you point through your mythologies and stories. Some of you point through the sciences. But all of your pointing to Source will never bring you to Source directly. That direct connection can only be experienced through a moment of awareness. And when in this awareness, you will be aware of the Love Force accepting and allowing all.

We've mentioned before that some of you are quite tired of the way this acceptance has played out in your creations. Your habituation to destruction and your defense against that destruction has been exhausting. Your destruction-based habits exhaust your resources, exhaust your emotional bodies, exhaust your well-being, exhaust the reservoirs of knowing who you are, exhaust your spiritual memory banks.

So a new choice has recently been made, and we wish now to explain how beliefs will either sustain and maintain this new choice—or put it to rest. We speak in a rather serious tone right now, for this is a profound choice before you: Do you choose a path which promotes well-being? Do you maintain the new choice to come back to your Selves? Do you choose to resurrect your spirits? Or will you see this grand choice before you and go back to maintain the habit of unbalanced destruction and defense and destruction and defense and destruction and defense …?

Beliefs will facilitate the choice and maintenance of either path.

Perhaps this is a good time to put forward how beliefs are created in the first place.

Beliefs are created as all creations are created: A thought-form arises of some kind. The thought-form is energized through experiences. As experiences occur, they start to coalesce into concepts. The concepts are further energized by your experiences and turn into beliefs. For instance, if you came to the planet as a small one who has been rejected by your mother and your father, your human-ness experiences a loss. The experience of loss might coalesce into the concept of abandonment and, with enough life experiences to energize this concept, turn into a belief, such as, "I cannot trust anyone because everyone will abandon me sooner or later."

The Golden Rule

Of course, this is but one of many beliefs which are formed within an individual. In order to create and maintain a path of well being for a planet of believers, may we suggest you cultivate compassion. Have compassion for all who believe whatever they believe and experience whatever they experience. Compassion will create well-being for yourself and others, rather than the creation of destructive habituation.

Instead of looking and pointing "out there" for what others can offer you, offer first to others how you would best be treated and honored. That is the golden rule of so many traditions and belief systems. You know the basics of this. You know the basics of treating another with respect for the other's conditions, choices, opportunities, even actions. So operating within that golden rule brings a more balanced structure to your lives, much as the golden mean is a cosmic rule, which promotes a balanced structure to the body of this Universe. This sounds rather complicated, and yet it is a very simple principle. See how there are universal principles at work which support balanced choices from the buffet table?

Examination of the World's Beliefs

An examination of your individual and collective beliefs has become popular. For instance, there is an increasing examination of the beliefs at work within your governing bodies. For now, all over the world, governance is based on a habitual way of thinking about life—with the corresponding belief that this habitual thinking is the correct way to govern. Without examination, this is indeed a quick path to destruction and the end of life on the planet.

There is also a burgeoning examination of the beliefs of those who govern. Many of you are asking: What beliefs do you "buy into"? What does not make sense to buy into? How can you collectively bring about governmental structures based on well-being? This will take a fair amount of sorting out. And yet it is within range in this age of choice to create government structures which promote well-being, the golden rule, and a balance of the forces of Creation and Destruction.

Other arenas where there will be the examination of beliefs include how you maintain the integrity of your bodies through the healing arts. A thorough review of what are now common treatment modalities will bring about a renaissance in healing and health maintenance.

As well, you will examine an arena we will discuss quite specifically: your economic flow (Living in a Post Consumer Economy, Chapter 15). What will be the baseline for future energy exchanges and monetary policies on this planet? As in all manner of human endeavors, beliefs run the economic show.

Every day, you are held entranced by the spell of your beliefs—every day. To acknowledge this truth will be very freeing for you. If you know you are so entranced by your beliefs, then you have the choice to wake up from the entrancement!

It is simple to wake up. Step into this awareness. You are conscious beings.

You are not just unconscious creatures thrashing around on this planet—far from it. That is how it seems, though, for you are so enchanted with your beliefs. The deeper examinations of your beliefs and the picking and choosing of which beliefs you wish to energize will allow a great shift in awareness, placing you all on a more benevolent path.

Several times in your day, experience this moment of conscious awakening—it only takes a moment. Ask yourself, "What do I believe right now? Does this belief work for me, work in my relationships, work for the benefit of others and the planet?"

When the great examination is truly in force—of your religious beliefs, sacred beliefs, political beliefs, beliefs about the physicality, beliefs on healing, beliefs about education, beliefs about economic engines, scientific beliefs, cultural beliefs—there will be daily wake-up calls for all of you, moment to moment to moment! You will collectively create support for your awakening. Education will support this awakening. Your values will support this awakening. Your path toward well-being will support this awakening.

So begin now. Begin the great examination. Start the exploration. Put on your pith helmets and enter the land of beliefs. See how beautifully and intricately they are structured—by you! And then, bit by bit, chip away at the structures that no longer serve you, and fully support and build upon the structures that do. From this exploration you will see the greatest change the world has ever experienced. You will have stepped onto the road of global well-being.

Beyond Belief: Archetypes

They gave me the option of ending this chapter as you've just read it or continuing with a further discussion, which seemed farther afield. I decided to include the rest of the download for those of you who might enjoy an exploration of what else we have created. Keep an open mind. It might be challenging to you, or not, but I think it is worth a look.

Archetypes

Are there any other details you wish to have us speak on today?

Thank you for your presence. What's been called the creator gods—I see culture so wrapped up within that mythology. Is that our creation as well? Are those gods a reflection of our own beliefs in an external source?

Would you like for us to hold forth on the creation of archetypes?

Yes. If this planet is cordoned off, one of the beliefs is that these super-beings come from elsewhere to affect the planet. If that's not the case, then are they our creations? Who are these creator gods we believe in anyway?

Let us state something very bluntly then, for the record. In order to bring a moment of clarity to this situation, you need to allow this in: YOU are the super-beings of which you speak. You are. Humanity is.

This all began—if there was a beginning—with a Consciousness of Oneness. Then there was the thought to separate into the One and the Other. From the Other sprang more others and more others and so on, to the creation of any and all others. This is the great mystery. There is no human way we can convey to you the incredible beauty that is the creation of something separate from the One.

There you have it. At first there was Oneness, then there was separation into an Other, and then all the others formed from that original separation. If you need to call that separation a fall, so be it. If you need to call it a creation, so be it. If you need to call it a spark, a big bang, or many different bangs, so be it, so be it, so be it! There is a great mystery there. But as far as this creation called planet Earth is concerned—yes, there were super beings who came to call. And they were you!

Yet who were the "others" who were here to play—the so-called creator gods? The Greek gods and goddesses, the European gods and goddess, the African gods and goddesses, the South American gods and goddesses, the aboriginal gods and goddesses, the great ones in the mythology of any of your people—all of these creations were formed in your minds to explain the forces of Consciousness. They were all a way to point to the One through the use of the Other. So, you are super-beings, can't you see? You're the ones creating and subscribing to your own beliefs.

On this planet of choice, you create your gods. You subscribe to your beliefs in them. You empower the beliefs; you energize your beliefs; you drop them; you change them; you manipulate them. You do not need any outside information or manipulation, thank you very much.

You do not even need to believe the very voice speaking to you now. For all you know, this voice is simply emanating from you. And in truth, we would rather you hear it this way. You called out to us who seem like a separate voice. Yet we are your voice. Hasn't it been true for you that some topics and issues you had been exploring on your own have come up in these discussions? So it is your voice that is speaking here! This is the voice of your super-being.

Archetypes are a way of putting order to your more persistent beliefs—and that is all. Humans are self-aware. Since self-awareness is the path for humanity, the archetypes fill in the details of the path. The archetypes demonstrate what the actions of, say, a hero might be or what the actions of a victim might be. They explore the actions of a person who has flaws and learns the lessons of those flaws, as well as the actions of a flawed person who has not learned from the flaws.

Archetypes were created in every single society of this planet. They've allowed you to set the stage for play. The great fascination on this planet has been, "How is this all going to turn out?" You love happy endings here. And yet, you also have a fascination with drama, with destruction for destruction's sake, with creation for creation's sake—sometimes all in one body.

To say that there has *not* been the influence of other beings from other systems would be a false statement. There has been. But the overriding momentum of choice has been humanity's alone. You've chosen what you've wanted to believe, in the form of archetypes you could learn from.

Is there such a thing as a Creator who is calling all the shots *for* you? In a word, no. However, is there a Creative Force, a Consciousness at work, in the creation of a planet and its inhabitants? Yes. Therefore we continue to say, Consciousness is at the basis of all.

Go and play with your archetypes, understand them, and make your choices as to whether you will empower them with your beliefs—or not! You can believe anything you wish. The choices are yours to make.

That is all for now.

The Universe is bending its ear to listen to your desires, your needs, your pleas, and your knowing.

Chapter 10

Have Faith

Please have faith in a conscious Universe, have faith in yourself, and have faith that you are creating your life in the best possible way under any circumstances. There is no worst possible way in the great scheme of things. Even when you are making a channel for the more bitter waters, you are still creating life in a conscious Universe.

The magic of this is that within a conscious Universe, you are always creating—see how powerful you are? What you so desire is yours—you cannot fudge that, you cannot fake that. If you are saying you want something, but in your heart of heart or soul of souls you do not truly desire it, then it is not in the flow of creation, and it will not be. So have faith in your true self and have faith in a conscious Universe awaiting your instructions.

Furthermore, we say to whoever is reading this and whoever is hearing this: You are in process. The world is in process. You are all processing how creations are created and how you will create the methods to reveal that heaven truly does exist on this planet. That is the great revelation of truth.

As much as you see the strife and horror, the pillaging of the earth's resources, we say to you that wherever there is an abundance of awful circumstances, there is an abundance of choice available to you. Now we aren't suggesting you shouldn't live a peaceful life on a peaceful earth and in harmony with your neighbor—that is what you are striving to do, is it not? Yet also know you have placed yourselves on a planet with a multitude of choices, an infinite amount of choices. You see before you the great variety of humans and how humans shape their cultures and experiences. You see how humans express and how each individual self is expressed. So have faith that these expressions are in process as well. Have faith in your process of creation. Have faith that you are well loved and attended to. The Universe is bending its ear to listen to your desires, your needs, your pleas, and your knowing.

You Are in Process.

Now we speak to how it is you will create a future everyone can live with. For the time is at hand when fear is ramped up and amped up, and this will continue for quite a few years beyond the point some people note to be the end of the world. For thousands of years there have been those who proclaim the end of the world is nigh, and yet you still see a world, do you not? So please understand that what you have created are numerous scenarios to bring on the end to a world as you know it. That is why you have created empires that have come and gone. Cultures have come and gone. Come and gone are thought-forms, beliefs, attitudes, what is proper and improper behavior. Whole worlds have come and gone on this planet—that is what's so fascinating about this planet of choice: There is a process always ongoing. Much as the ebb and flow of the ocean waves shape a shoreline, the ebb and flow of your thoughts usher in tidings of doom and discontent as well as tidings of possibility and opportunity, which constantly shape the contours of your lives.

As you might notice in your media cultures, there are plenty of visions of a not-so-happy future. Planet-wide, your media often pictures the future as one of doom and gloom. These darker thoughts need to be expressed, however—while in a process, expression is important. When one is processing a death, when one is processing important life events, expression in all its variety and of the light and the dark thoughts is quite important. However, we ask you: Which of those expressions do you actually wish to create? Do you wish to create a world bereft of life or a world of struggle and strife and worldwide war and barely surviving every day? You already have plenty of that, dear people.

There are opportunities to express your dualistic nature while still creating a world for all.

For example, in the great spiritual traditions, there is plenty of opportunity for a multitude of expressions in the form of colorful beliefs: In Hinduism, the religious tradition of the ten thousand gods, there is the expression of destruction in Kali, the expression of war in Shiva, the expression of peace in Krishna, and the expression of so much wisdom in Ganesha, etc. There is wisdom to honoring expression in its varying forms. For those traditions that have the one-God approach there is also a wealth of differing expressions: There can be an expression of a jealous God, an expression of a tender God, an expression of a loving God; there is a wise God as well as a God of revenge. There is wisdom in this expression as well, for what these gods reflect are human consciousness and, most important, what human consciousness wishes to express. So there is wisdom and plenty of space in this world to express all.

You Are Creating. You Are Destroying.

Why is it you express in ways damaging to the Earth and to each other? Well this is another great mystery, yet we will try to explain: From the beginning of this earth's life, a pulse from Creation was sent out with a special intention for this planet of choice: to allow the full exploration of Destruction's expression in equal measure with Creation's expression. As we've stated in another conversation with you, Destruction is just as important as Creation.

In your future, you will have great destruction, but what is it you will actually destroy? Perhaps you will destroy the roots of hatred. Perhaps you will destroy the seeds bearing bitter fruits of war. Perhaps you destroy structures which do not sustain humanity or the planet itself as you allow your economic structures and other structures of maintaining a life go by the wayside. Right now it's only the beginning of this.

In the meantime there are new creations, which are mere seeds now. These tiny, tiny seeds, sprinkled throughout the human population, bear the potential for a new way of being on the planet. Amongst you are the few people exploring just what the seeds can create, allowing the seeds to sprout here and there. Their imaginative minds use the resources at hand to create a life worth living for all.

No matter what you create, there is no ultimate judgment as to how much or how little resources you use on the planet. Some beings require more resources than others—that is just a simple fact. For instance, an elephant requires more food than a mosquito. Relatively speaking for its weight, a hummingbird requires a huge amount of resources. So, too, in the human form, there are some who have and use more resources than others. Our point is, no matter how much you are working with, all of you can come to the table to share your gifts and contribute to the whole. Break through the illusion that you need to have a certain amount of knowledge, monetary wealth, or special physical attributes or spiritual prowess to create your desires.

No matter who you are or how you express, you all create thusly:

A thought-form arises out of nothing. The thought-form expands and gains some momentum and energy. How this is gained is somewhat of a mystery, yet you know that when you have an idea that has gained energy you sense the possibility of creation when it is time to act. So, too, it is with all thought-forms—when they gain momentum, they also gain energy and are eventually created. The creation then has a life span that may be a second, a millisecond, a year, many years, a millennium etc. Some created structures live longer because of the amount of energy given to them. This is why certain cultural norms have been around for centuries if not thousands of years—they are supported by the energy of a culture's thought-forms.

Yet some thought-forms are birthed and immediately die. How is that determined? Thought-form creation and life span are determined by both individual human thoughts and by how others support the thoughts. For instance if the human is accustomed to paying attention to and creating out of the culture one lives in, this affects the human's thought-forms. Let's say a woman in a culture which supports the treatment of women in a certain way wishes to be treated differently—this is her seed-thought-form. Yet she also experiences her culture treating her in ways other than her desire: She might create resentment, and she might create quiet anger—she might create all kinds of thoughts but not necessarily an obvious change.

Let's say the tension between the woman's desires and the thought-forms of her culture creates its own energy. That energy gains momentum and more energy, and perhaps other people contribute their thoughts on the matter and act on those thoughts. Eventually, when there is enough energy to break the tension, a change in the treatment of women occurs.

Even with some of the dramatic changes in beliefs and attitudes over the ages, there is still the residue of old energy. But the changes persist even though the old energy still reverberates through human consciousness. For instance, in the USA and Europe, slavery is highly frowned upon, and so you do not see much of it there—that has been the truth of the matter for a while. The miracle is that any change happens at all. The miracle of this planet is that changes are created by your thought-forms. Eventually enough momentum and energy are put into the new forms that a change has to happen—the tension is too much for the old structure to stay strong. The old structure crumbles, the new thought-forms finally take hold.

Consciousness and the great revealing of conscious awareness are the miracles of modern day. You would not have the technology, you would not have the abundance of what you have today without a blossoming awareness—you would not. Why is this? Because with each level of awareness in humanity, that change in awareness moves through the cultures and spreads worldwide, giving more and more people the opportunity to energize the change.

Many things are created more quickly now than in years back because more people are consciously on board in their desire for change. In those places where people want to stay in the old energy and not change, they will scuffle and fight for survival—and there has to be an allowance for the egos to fully express themselves. This may sound like a cruel thing—people in war zones do not deserve to be in war zones—absolutely not. Yet people in current war zones will be tremendous change agents in the future. Since they are in zones where old energy is so entrenched, when the breakthrough happens, it will be like the breaking of a dam holding back a very full lake. The waterfall of cascading change will be immense.

In places such as the Middle East, the people hold onto an ancient hateful energy. Once that energy breaks free, walls will literally crumble by the people's choice. From this choice, you will see a great change all over the earth, including in great lands where enslavement still dampens the human spirit and blocks the creative impulse of the soul. The Middle East is a relatively small area of the world, is it not? Yet once the enslavement to hatred there breaks free, you will see a tremendous amount of healing energy beamed around the world.

Never underestimate the power of small change—so perceived only in your mind's eye. Never underestimate the change you have on the world when you change but one undesirable habit. Never underestimate your changing of the thought-forms which do not support you. All of these changes contribute to the whole in great measure—more than you would ever believe. We ask you to have faith in this process and to have faith in yourself and what it is you can do to affect change. You can affect change in private, you can affect change in public—in the great scheme of things it does not matter. You are the ones creating the thoughts; you are the ones energizing the thoughts. You are allowing them to emerge into the creations of your dreams.

Meanwhile create heaven in your own corner of the world. The best way you can create heaven and heavenly thoughts is not just to look up to a heaven located somewhere off-planet. Heaven follows you wherever you are, even if the world looks bleak all around. Take heaven with you; place it in your life-journey's knapsack. Create heaven with your intentions, with your attention, with your smiles, but especially with the magic of your grateful heart. For every grateful thought and every grateful act, you can change hundreds of negative thought-forms. Every act of gratitude affects thousands of people.

As you sit by the ocean of opportunity, be in gratitude for the ebb and flow of abundant resources. Be in gratitude for the opportunities to cleanse the ocean, returning it to its natural state, to heal that which was deathly ill, to create a world you can all thrive in. Have faith in yourself, in your creativity, and especially your ability to be grateful for all.

And that is all for now.

It is time to see each other differently. It is time to honor the Christ within all.

Chapter 11

Maintaining the Integrity of Your Intentions

When you arrive on this earth plane, you have every good intention to bring your special gifts with you. During your life-spans, it is then a matter of attempting to act out of that intention and align with your purpose. Yet, doesn't it feel as if some of your good intentions get lost in translation from spirit-life to earth-life?

So with compassion and affection for our fellow, well-intended spirits, we wish to talk about maintaining the integrity of your intention. Maintaining your spirit's intentions has been quite a daunting task as you have attempted to make your way on your life pathway as both a human and as an adventurous spirit.

Maintaining the integrity of your intention will be the watchwords, the theme, of the Shift in the ages to come. The Shift is already occurring now, for is it not so that integrity is being challenged left and right? On the left side and the right side and in the vast middle of humanity's persuasions, there is a challenge to the integrity of an individual's choices and actions and the integrity of a group's choices and actions. The challenges have come; but there is some skepticism as to whether there will be any permanent change via the challenges. And yet we are delighted to announce that right now, right here, on this very planet, a choice has been made within the consciousness of humanity to maintain the integrity of your greater collective intention.

And what is that greater intention? It is to awaken to your true Self and your true place in the cosmos as an energy-being, creating an energy pathway every moment of your day. You are awakening to your power to create an energy pathway towards integrity and well-being for ALL players on this planet and in the greater Universe. We cannot say enough how much we honor you for this.

For so long, humanity as a mass consciousness has habituated to the energy of destruction and the corresponding defense against destruction. This habitual energy of defense and destruction and defense and destruction has allowed for moments of creation as well, since creation is occurring all the time. This habitual patterning has allowed for the creation of unbalanced destruction, and yet there have been times when you've also allowed the more conscious creations of well-being and balance. And, therefore, you still sit or stand here as a human being. If those choices to consciously create well-being were not made—however infrequently they occurred—then you would not be here, and that would be that.

You've had many opportunities for destruction of the planet and humanity. As the main player on Earth, this ultimate choice was yours to make as you were left to your own devices.

Yet, even as you've recently witnessed millions of people crossing over to the other side via wars, earth changes, and other forms of destruction, we remind you that there is no absolute destruction of any one being—not a one! All are spared; all are called to the table of abundant Love. All are asked to review their actions and intentions, and all are celebrated for the attempt to make their way on the Earth.

Now there is a conscious choice made by enough people to maintain the integrity of the greater intention of awakening. Do you understand this? Can you let that in? Can you feel the impact of this loving choice you have collectively made?

It may seem as if the times of darkness are still upon you, and in so many ways, that will seem true for quite some time. Yet the glimmerings of light are occurring within the individuals who are choosing to maintain the integrity of their intentions by aligning their actions with their purpose.

So, how to maintain the integrity of your intention? First up is to know that you *have* intentions! Ask yourself every day, several times in the day: What is your intention for any action? You might also ask: What are you paying attention to; what are you pouring your energy into?

With an awareness of your intentions, you will notice intentions that do not serve you, your purpose, or your well-being. This will become quite obvious to you. The awareness of these lesser intentions will spur you to climb out of your habitual boxes of destruction and the concurrent defense against destruction.

So, be aware of your intentions first. Armed with an awareness of your "lesser" intentions, choose not to empower them—give them no energy. They have emerged, you've examined them, and now you choose to go for the greater intentions. By "greater" we mean in greater alignment with your purpose. Furthermore, as you are aware of your greater intentions, you will choose to take actions which support them. Do you understand?

Your mind, your emotions, and your body may respond one way or another to the greater or lesser intentions and to the actions that spring from those intentions. So pay attention to your body. If your body is in a state of degradation, and you feel this, examine your actions—and mostly examine your intentions.

If the reaction to aligning with your greater purpose is a flutter in your solar plexus, in your stomach, then that is fear arising and asking to have its say. And you will allow fear to have its say, for your fearful thoughts and your fearful emotions are there to teach you about what you are habituated to. We say to you with a smile: Have no fear of your fear! Have no fear of your doubts. And especially, have no fear of your reactions, for they are all great teachers. If you do not know what you fear, then it is very difficult for you to maintain the integrity of your intentions.

So there is an awareness of your intention. There is an awareness of the lesser intentions and the choices made not to empower them. There is an awareness of your greater intentions, with greater alignment to your purpose. There is the acknowledgement of the reactions within your energy field, your emotional field, and your physical field.

Amazing Grace

There is also the awareness of when you are in the flow of honoring your greater intention. When you are in integrity with this intention, you will remember the greater spirit you are and always will be. You will experience a moment of grace.

This is our greatest wish for humanity: That you experience this moment of grace more and more often. Look for this. Look for the moments, the minutes, the hours, the days, the weeks, the years of grace!

Look to those people who experience grace as an everyday state of being, no matter what circumstances they find themselves in: a moment of grace while they're dying, a moment of grace while they're crying, a moment of grace while they're in the flow of acting on their purpose.

Role models of grace are everywhere. Look for them, and look to them. In them you will see the true meaning of the resurrection and the return of a Christ: It is the return of you—all of you—to your true Selves. It is time to see each other differently. It is time to honor the Christ within all.

One of the great masters has said, "The kingdom of heaven is within you." And that kingdom supports the maintenance of the integrity of your greater intentions, your wisdom, your knowing, your grace, and dare we say, your joy. This planet, though left to its own devices, is a planetary paradise. You need look no further than this actual planet of choice. You made the choices you've made. Now honor them and release them. You've had your intentions played out in any given lifetime: Honor those, and release them.

It is in your integrity to create a world of abundant grace. Even though the defenses are stepped up among some, even as the darkness descends upon the great many, there is always darkness before dawn. It is wise to accept the darkness for what it is: a reminder of how you have forgotten yourselves and how the Great Remembrance—the resurrection many of you have been waiting for—is upon you.

We say one more thing. Don't be fooled.

Don't be fooled by those who wish to maintain separation and unbalanced destruction. Allow them to play out their game, for they have their purpose, too. Yet, don't be fooled by them. Don't buy in and energize the forgetful habits of these dear souls.

The dawn of your new day is upon you. Enjoy it. And breathe in our delight in your accomplishment.

Thank you for your kind attention to our loving intention.

And that is all for now.

It is time to ... listen to the quieter voice within humanity's collective soul.

Chapter 12

Attention and Listening

What do you pay attention to?

If there is a lone baby in a household, and a parent hears the baby cry, the parent is apt to pay attention, run to the baby, and try to fulfill the baby's needs until the baby ceases to cry. Yet, if within a crowded noisy home, the baby's cry is not heard, then there is less likelihood for a parent or anyone to pay attention and fulfill the baby's needs.

So, too, it is with humanity's cries: What is often created is from listening to the louder "voices" amongst the din of thought-forms. A louder voice is paid attention to by the parent-control of the mind, and there is this tendency to want to fulfill a perceived need in order to still the cry.

There's a saying among people: The squeaky wheel gets the oil—or the squeaky wheel gets the attention. So, too, it is within humanity's hue and cry. Thus, the attempts by peoples on all sides of an issue to cry louder than anyone else! In any given country, on any given day, there are cries on both sides of a debate on any number of issues.

People surmise the louder the cry, the more they're apt to get attention. This is often true. Yet with all the din, how is anything of consequence accomplished? In a crowded field of problems begging for attention, how will you all know what is most important to attend to?

So we would like to speak to listening.

It is time to listen to the still, small voice within a person's soul and listen to the quieter voice within humanity's collective soul. That voice will transcend the loud voices, which stir up dust and do not allow people to see the heart of each issue.

The loud voices of humanity have held sway for quite some time, haven't they? When you view older film footage, you need only hear the speeches by some of the orators of your time. The louder voices were the ones most apt to be listened to! For example, when Hitler gave his speeches to the people of WWII Germany, he was literally yelling—and people listened. He had a stern countenance, as if he was that stern father figure who knew what was best for everybody and what to warn "the children" against.

Even people who had the best interest of their culture in mind had a tendency to speak loudly. Now, some of this had to do with acoustics—in the olden days, there were no such things as microphones—we acknowledge that. Yet there was also something gained by using that louder voice—people pay attention to a baby's loud cry or a father's or mother's stern warnings and expressions of fear for the safety of the children. And so in humanity's continuing struggle to evolve within a dualistic perspective, the louder voices have often held the attention of the mass culture.

One of the loudest voices in mass culture is the voice we'll name drama. Drama speaks loudly, shrilly, and draws to itself massive attention—if even for a moment. Dramatic events are all the rage in your news programming and even in this day and age of instant information via the Internet. The more dramatic the voice, the more attention it is apt to gain in the population.

Humanity is in love with drama, as if drama is a god to be worshipped and paid attention to or as if drama is that crying child who needs attention. Now in the larger scheme of things, there is a benefit to this: You cannot correct and change issues you do not hear about. If the drama of a situation is not brought out for the public to perceive, there cannot be any change in that arena in the moment the drama is happening. It is often in retrospect, when there are toxic results from the drama, that people actually begin to examine how the drama unfolded in the first place.

Yet notice how often that examination does not occur until *several* dramas take place after the original drama.

In the example of the events of 9–11–2001, there was the initial drama: the attack on certain edifices of the United States. There was the ensuing triage and treatment and care-giving of those who needed caring for. There was the further stirring up of drama by wondering how to protect and defend against more attacks of this nature.

And then further drama upon that drama, the attack was countered with more attacks. Wars were created, attacks against whole cultural groups were enacted, and suspicions were high of just about anyone out of the "norm."

None of the seeds of the original drama of 9–11 were closely examined until quite a few years after that drama. Whereas, if there had been an immediate call to examine just what it was that sourced and led up to that dramatic point in humanity's history, other choices might have been made to attend to that loud cry heard around the world.

For instance, if the seeds of that drama were seen to be the impoverishment and the slave consciousness of whole cultures of people, you would also see that these people needed somewhere to point in rage so they might feel at least a shred of power. Different actions might have been taken to quell those needful voices with an examination of what needs were met by this attack.

There are many other examples of dramas that humans have attended to with further drama. Even the way you treat illness as a drama to be fixed with more drama is rather interesting. There are very few who seek out the root thoughts, the root cause, the root events and beliefs, which led up to the actual illness or pandemic. Rather, wars are waged; battle lines are drawn. There is a war against drug use. There is a war against cancer. There is a war against AIDS. You get our point.

We have no judgment about this way of engaging drama. Yet we do suggest that engaging drama with more drama will further that drama and keep it activated. There is an opportunity here for you to step back and discover what combination of thoughts, actions, or perceptions were present to create the drama in the first place. You can then attend to the drama so discoveries are made and lessons are learned.

Law of Attention

That which is given the most attention will be that which is created. This is the law of attention. The law of attention states that whatever one most pays attention to—whether it's a drama, an incident, a belief, an action, or even a mere thought—will eventually gain enough energy to be manifested in the world. For instance, if there is a fear of falling stock markets, then attention will be given to statements such as, "Good fortune never lasts," or "I'm going to get mine before the fall," or "Live today, for tomorrow we'll be broke." Any variation on a theme of falling is energized by the constant attention to that possibility, leading to its probable manifestation. Do you understand?

Thus fear, being a louder voice than the voices of balance or perspective, draws attention to itself, threatening the very survival of the one feeling the fear.

That is why fear creates stress in a body, and the stress creates a receptacle for illness. Then further energizing that illness is the attack on the illness, for the illness is now to be feared. And even if there is a temporary cure of that illness, the illness's imprint is kept alive by the attention to the original fear.

Fear is the most prominent reaction to any given situation where a human feels out of control. Fear gets the attention, whether fear deserves it or not! Gone is the attention to what is working. Vanished is the attention to gratitude, to wholeness, to balance—and to Creation. It is quite difficult to create anything other than fear when one's attention is on fear and drama.

Your examination of the effects of fear and drama on humanity's consciousness will yield tremendous breakthroughs in humanity's evolution. Examining the roots of your fears will yield an abundance of information about how the dramas were created in the first place. Everything from the roots of human illnesses to the stresses on all systems of the planet will be discovered through this deep analysis. There is no better time than the present to examine how attention to fear and drama directly correlates with the survival of these dramas and problems.

Within any given time in humanity's history, why has there been a war of some sort somewhere in the world? Because the original drama, which sparked a disagreement that blossomed into a full-out war, was not examined. Without the examination of the root cause of any skirmish, the skirmish will just continue with devilish persistence, draining energy and creativity and resources from a culture's coffers.

Some say that wars were created by one person or another. A leader caused a war. But that could not be further from the truth. Leaders do not cause wars. They only continue to feed upon the attention paid to the drama that is already being played out. They are people who love to play on these dramas, so they keep people enslaved to a constant state of fear and even terror. And the people who listen to these leaders keep the drama alive.

We cannot stress this point enough; if attention is paid to the drama and the fear which the drama produces, that keeps the drama alive and thriving! All sorts of dramas are fed by this attention: personal dramas, emotional dramas, physical dramas, psychological dramas, as well as group dramas, cultural skirmishes, prejudice, bigotry, hatred of anyone different from one's own way of life, and even global dramas, such as the dramas of imbalance in the world's ecosystems, as well as large-scale cultural hatreds and defenses. Your attention to these dramas is almost to the point of affection for being in drama—and the terrible mess you are in and how it is too complex and too entrenched to solve. Very few of these dramas have the corresponding attention paid to creative solutions.

Humanity is in love with the familiar. You gravitate towards people who seem to think like you do. You gravitate towards familiar situations, even if the situations are unhealthy or toxic. And so an initial abusive relationship will spawn further abusive relationships, and so on, and so on, through generations. All based on this affection for familiarity.

Listen

You might be wondering: Now what?

How should you hold all the current dramas in the world and in your personal and community lives? May we suggest you hold these dramas very tenderly, with compassion, as one would hold a terrified child waking up from a bad dream. One does not scold a young one for having a nightmare. One might hold the scared one in a comforting embrace, which states, "You are safe now." And then one makes an attempt to show the child that, indeed, all is well in the moment.

So, too, might humanity hold drama in an embrace that comforts, striving to pay attention in a way which does not foster more drama and in a way that states in the moment, "All is well."

Deep listening is what is needed to quell the sniffling, fearful emotion that drama brings to the face of humanity. So ask first, "What are you experiencing?" Then listen to the answer, noting and embracing what is true for any given person or culture. Only after deep listening occurs can the question of what might possibly resolve the drama be asked. After that question is asked, deeply listen to the answers, for there will be multiple answers as to what might resolve any drama. Then an actual plan for resolution may be proposed and acted upon.

The law of attention states that if people attend to solution and possibility, then the possibility for solution will be created. So pay attention to the dramas most certainly for they are the cries of ones who need attention. And then, through active listening to what the source thoughts and perceptions are for any given drama, start to shift the attention to the possibility of solution. Naturally, "practice makes perfect," as they say; so put into practice the solutions that work for any given situation.

Act on a solution which arises from deep listening, and see if it works! If the solution is not really a solution, creative people listen some more to determine what is working and what simply is not. Attention paid to resolution, combined with the determination to stay on that forwarding track, will eventually resolve the original seed-drama, as well as the recurring dramas which grew from the seed.

The more and more attention paid to that which nurtures, that which brings joy and a sense of well-being, the more humans will yearn for a persistence of these states of being. And the more they will withdraw their attention from that which brings unease, disease, and pain.

Take a breath, humanity, and then take another deep breath.

Be still for a moment, and stop the shouting.

Listen to your innermost heart's yearnings, and place your attention there.

Celebrate your differences of perception. Celebrate your colorful ways of thriving. One of the greatest secrets on the planet is that most people seek the same things: joy, comfort, love and attention from another, having a purpose. These are but a few of the common yearnings of each and every human being. Yet because your attention is on the louder, more divisive voices, the quieter voices have only a limited voice at the table.

So take a breath and then another. And listen. Listen. Humanity's vast potential is about to be tapped. And it starts with tapping into your very own.

That is all for now.

Regardless of the conditions you find yourself in, the power of choice is still with you.

Chapter 13

Chaos and the Eye of the Storm

The journey of living upward in Consciousness is often the passage through the eye of a storm. How do you navigate your life through a stormy sea that seems filled with fear, hostility, paranoia, constraint, lies, and manipulation?

Let us use the metaphor of hurricanes or cyclones—for they shall be increasing in number and intensity. If you are at the edge of the storm, you are exposed to the destructive power of the wind and water. But if you are in the eye of the storm, it is, paradoxically, calm. Even with the turmoil all around you, in your center, all is still.

From our perspective you must find within yourself the center point of the storm. There is no one who can teach you this. There is no one who can save you from the storms that are upon you. You will experience both the external storms of your weather, politics, economics, and earth changes, as well as the internal storms of your psychological and emotional conflicts as you navigate a world that is quickly dissolving into a new world. There is little solid ground here, and such states of transition can be anxiety-provoking.

Most of you have not learned how to dance with chaos in a gracious manner, but don't be concerned about this. For soon you shall have many dance lessons and opportunities to be at peace with the partner of chaos and its swirling uncertainty.

In these times, it will be easier to surrender to a downward spiral than to live upward. And yet living upward in Consciousness is why you are here in this time. The essential point is that this is a time to rise upward in yourself and walk the higher spiritual ground. There is a battle taking place within you for your very spirit, heart, and mind. It's time to find the spiritual courage not to succumb to the downward spiral, to find a way to live upward in yourself, even in the midst of increasing chaos, difficulties, and seeming disasters.

We say seeming disasters because the events, such as catastrophes, storms, famine, loss of jobs, and so on, are multi-dimensional in nature. Certainly from the perspective of a physical self locked into time and space, these events are varying degrees of awful. Yet from the standpoint of your multidimensional self—your true Self—these events are opportunities for immense growth and an acceleration of spiritual evolution.

There is a tendency for humans to repeat old patterns. This is based upon expectations, which are based on your experiences. It is possible to cut through your patterns, but this is done through the door of Consciousness only you can open. It is done through both personal intent and action.

When you find yourself disheartened, disillusioned, disconnected, and with no desire for your life, realize you have simply wandered through one of the doors of your own self-limited consciousness. In these moments of recognizing you are in a lower vibratory expression of your potential, seize the moment, and step out of that doorway in order to choose another path.

The difficulties some of you may be experiencing may seem to preclude any choice in your outer reality. Yet, regardless of the conditions you find yourself in, the power of choice is still with you because the power of choice resides within you. In your most difficult moments, when all doors seem closed, all that is required to change a situation is a small movement in consciousness. As you build upon this movement, vast powers within you are released. Yet until you have movement within you of some kind, nothing will change.

So this is our suggestion for how to create a small movement within you when everything else has failed: Even in the midst of personal torment, external difficulties, and whatever presents itself to you as a problem, find something to appreciate.

It might be as simple as appreciating your breath, or something that made you laugh. What is important here is that when all options are closed, if you find something to feel appreciation for—no matter how small—you have created a small movement in consciousness. With that movement, great things will unfold.

Some will ride the storms more gracefully than others. Yet even those considered spiritually evolved may be challenged from time to time as the old world dissolves into something new. Some of you will be caught in the grips of the chaotic times; yet it is our hope and desire for you to recall our simple suggestion: Remember to find something to appreciate.

That is all for now.

*If you are conscious of what problems you have created,
then you can be just as conscious of the solutions.*

Chapter 14

The Future Is in Your Present

There may be those of you, as our co-creators in Consciousness, who wish to take advantage of representatives such as we are for the higher Selves in order to ask us the following question: "What is in our future?"

And we answer with this: The future is already in your present. It is now. The future is in your presence as well. It is here. And for those of you who love the play of words, the future is already within your presents (with the English spelling, p-r-e-s-e-n-t-s). So in your present times, and within the presents (the gifts) you hold, may we present to you this fact: Every single problem and situation of grief and division you have on this planet has a corresponding solution.

These solutions are not only slated to appear in your future when you might be on the final brink of destruction, moments before it's too late for humanity. You are already on the brink. And what you are on the brink of is discovery—revealing the answers for the problems and situations you have co-created with a conscious Universe. Co-creation equals creation in cooperation with an attentive Universe. Co-creation is happening here, now.

We have discussed the process of creation. Now, we wish to speak of the process of *conscious* creation—consciously creating what you actually wish to see in the world. For quite some time, you have utilized the forces of Creation, Destruction, Love, and Essence to create what you might call a crisis or a problem or "Help! We don't want to do this anymore!"

But here's the gift: If you are conscious of what problems you have created, then you can be just as conscious of the solutions.

We'll speak more directly about how to find solutions to problems, which have plagued humanity for quite some time. Before we go there, we need to insert into this discussion that we have no judgment about your creations. Please, please understand that. There is no judgment on our parts or the Universe's part or Creator's part or Creation's part and definitely not on Love's behalf. There is nary a hint of judgment here as to any creations you have created.

However, *you* have judgments about your creations, do you not? You have judgments about personal, global, and community-wide creations; creations of pollution; creations of stripping the earth of its resources; creations of poisoned air, land, and water, and so on. But again we say that for each of these created problems, you have also the solutions to the problems—though they might seem hidden from your view. Remember, the future is in your presence—it's here, now. The future is also in the presents and gifts you unwrap to reveal creative solutions for whatever ails you.

Why are the solutions hiding? Do these solutions not want to be discovered? Are they playing hide-and-seek? Well, in a sense, there is truth in this. They are hiding from your view because you are simply not aware of them. And they are playing hide-and-seek because you are seeking them out now, more and more.

Nature's Solutions

The solutions to the problems and the answers to your more persistent queries are everywhere. One area your solutions are hidden is within the observation of nature. For instance, solutions can be found in the observation of the tides and the ebb and flow of an ocean. There are solutions from observing how all of the physical elements work so beautifully together. There are hints within natural patterns and the seasons. There are hints within each ecological community and system.

You push the boundaries of nature, bending nature to your will, only to have nature snap right back. In order to find the solutions to some of your more persistent problems, work with nature and you will find many, many, many answers. For instance, you will find answers in plant life for diseases. You will find answers in the cyclical nature of nature to other physical problems. You will know how to support and sustain this world and how to be good stewards of this planet and how to use natural resources to their maximum ability and your maximum desire to live a life of balance.

Within nature, you will find answers for issues of balance and being off balance: Observe patterns whenever a storm blows through an area or whenever an earthquake shakes the roots of a culture for there are solutions in the patterns. Nature occasionally speaks loudly, yet oftentimes softly. Nature has within its very complex anatomy all the solutions for your complex anatomy. So be observant and be present for the presents nature offers you.

The Answers in the Fields

There has been a trend on the planet for approximately thirty of your years (at the time of this discussion): An encoded language is being transmitted right in front of your collective faces. The answers to so many human-made problems are in the fields.

The designs in the fields are created by a conscious intelligence—your consciousness blended with universal Consciousness and the intelligence of this Earth. This combining of Consciousness and intelligence is creating designs in the agricultural fields of what is now called Great Britain and occasionally in other places on the Earth, as well as every once in a while in the skies. These crop designs have been witnessed by millions in person and via various forms of media, yet you still do not know what to do with them! There are many people who are in denial of the intelligence behind these designs. It would do you a great service to pay attention to the designs and decode them, using your brightest, most imaginative minds, for within them you'll discover solutions to your most persistently awful cares and woes.

You will note that in some of the patterns there are repeated designs. The circle is a sign of completion and wholeness. The spiral is a sign of evolution and the fact that everything in the Universe is created, has a life span, and has its dissolution back into the oneness. And so the spiral is both creation and evolution. You might ask: An evolution of what? Well, there's evolution of all the beings who've been on this planet. There's an evolutionary process in the Universe itself and even in humanity's conscious intelligence. (We are collectively "winking" at you right now, demonstrating that within the pattern of the spiral there is joy! Note how that pattern can bring joy to a person just by looking at it!)

There are patterns that recreate designs within nature itself, pointing to the answers that lie there. There are also patterns and designs that point to answers you have *already* come up with. Humans the world over can attest to, every once in a while, having an insight of some kind. Some insights come from "out of the blue," and some have persisted for a long time, pulling you to action. Some ideas about the messages within the crop designs will come from "out of the blue," and some ideas are already harbored within people's hearts. Perhaps it will take a number of people examining a design and coming up with their insightful interpretations.

Can you recall at least once in your life when the answer simply "arrived"? This is not just a rhetorical question. The reason for the answer's arrival is an opening to an awareness of both problem and solution, to an awareness of both human and being, to an awareness of both microcosm (you and your small world) and the macrocosm. In this moment of insight, you are aware of how you and your small world are an integral part of the greater world.

Look for patterns in the beautiful designs. Look for patterns within nature. Within these patterns, look for sequencing, and look for mathematical formulas. In the mathematical formulas, you will see what is in balance and what is off-kilter in your personal universe. In the patterns, you'll find answers for healing medical situations, as well as for healing pollution, including nuclear pollution and extreme toxic waste.

Everything can be dealt with in balance. Energize the thought that the answers are already present. You need only to seek them out.

The Future of Education Is Here

Here is another look into the future already present within you: There are children on the planet, as well as those arriving in the next numbers of years, who are born with their intuition and telepathy fully intact—and they will not want to shut these down. So be aware of this trend and prepare yourselves. Except for a very few, your institutions are not in any way prepared for these children.

Look for solutions to education—they are already here. There are bright minds out there, people who are in balance with their intuition and their intellect and their physicality. They instinctively know the individual gifts these children have to share with the planet. In the future education of children, you will find ways of bringing out their gifts, their presence, their knowing. Look for the patterns within the children already present: What do you see as natural for them? They all wish to learn; they want to explore; they want to know. Yet their senses are dulled down by the world you have collectively created and by the forms of education you have collectively created. Again, we are not saying this to you with judgment; we are just stating what is so.

Solutions in education for all are here among the people—just ask some of the bright minds. Ask for solutions from people who have a passion for teaching *anything*: "Why do you want to teach what you wish to teach? How do you want to teach it? How do you want to present this knowledge? Do you want to present this physically? Do you want to engage a pupil in an internship format? Do you want them to sit? Do you want them to stand? Do you want them to sing? How will they absorb the information? What will they do with the information?" All these questions are never asked in most schooling situations. And yet the solutions for education will come through answering these questions—bringing a whole new way of being with not only your children, but with yourselves as you learn.

A great majority of people choose to be experiential learners. They choose experiences over books. They will dive headlong into an experience—even a painful experience—in order to be educated about their boundaries or lack thereof; to understand what makes them sick or what brings them to health; to discover more and more about how they operate in the world. All manner of answers are within the experiences of people! So be your own best observer. Observe how much you are present and how much of the time you are not present. Observe and ask: Why do you elect to have certain experiences? Experiences rarely happen by accident. Experiences flow through your life for your education and your growing in wisdom. You experience what you need to learn and where you need to grow.

Energy Pathways

Here is another present you have in abundance in your present time: telepathy, or the ability to communicate with and understand communication from an animal, another human being, or a group of human beings. Right now, you also have the ability within every one of you to know what is happening anywhere—even thousands of miles from where you sit or stand or read this or listen to this. There are methodologies people are developing to access this gift.

You were never meant to be quite so closed to the information all around you as you are now. Your forgetting who you are blocks your ability to access the information. You have the abilities, the gifts, and the mechanisms right now to be in touch with anyone on the planet without the use of any devices or technology. No electricity needed. No antennae or satellite. No microwaves. You need only tune into the wave upon wave upon wave of frequency each of you is emitting and everything and every being on this world is emitting.

For now, we'll call these frequency emissions "energy pathways." In order for you to understand other human beings and how they are playing on this planet of choice, all you need to do is to tune into their energy pathway. Ask: What is the path they are creating? Not just the physical pathway but also the pathways in their minds, the pathway of their evolution, the pathway their choices create. If you can but tune into a culture's energy pathway, you will have an abundance of ways to communicate with that culture in a way that is in balance, non-aggressive, and in complete understanding—even if the culture is very different from your own.

And so it is with another human being. If you will understand even a small slice of the pathway, you might understand who he or she is and why that person has made the choices he or she has made. You will have compassion for this human. The same goes for animals, the same goes for a piece of land; the same goes for this entire earth—all can be understood and attended to by an understanding of energy pathways.

Suffice it to say without going into a great discourse (because we can speak of this topic for hours), there are those among you who understand the theory of energy pathways and have the gifts of accessing and reading the frequencies of people. We also state that right here, right now, there are healing methods using frequency alone. The methods utilize the emission of frequency pulses without the use of an electrical source. With what you literally have on hand, you can heal just about everything there is to be healed within the human form, as well as within the forms that are off-balance in this planet.

For instance, there are people who have used frequency and sound to change the ph of overly acidic water, as well as clean up polluted water. This has already been achieved. With the judicious use of frequency, your future is in your presence. By the way, we are not saying do not ever use technology-oriented mechanisms—technology has its place. But technology is not the solution to all your persistent problems. It is not. Technology without wisdom is a path to death. This you have witnessed for quite some time, have you not?

So may we recommend: Use a balance of both your natural resources and technology. Everything you need is on your person already. However, in the evolution of humanity, you've created technologies in order to further your understanding. For instance, you use the Internet and other devices to communicate instantly with people far, far away—and this is all very good. Yet, there will be a time in your near future—and already in the presence of the gifted few—when instant communication will occur regularly without the use of any technology.

For now, however, there are people with a variety of gifts and desires. There are gifts within people who love to create technology, as well as those who love to use the forces of nature. Some people like to use their own hands or eyes or bodies; and some people like to use their brains. Some people beam a frequency of love. There are among you healers who do nothing but sit in meditation, thereby healing themselves and healing the planet. Are you aware of this?

All these gifts of the future are in your present, within the presence of these people. Look to them; have them teach you their secrets because they will, in turn, reveal this secret:

You are the answer to your problems. You are. Your presents (your gifts) and your presence in the now is all you need.

And that is all for now.

If an economy was seen as an entity that promotes well-being, you would have a distinctively different world.

Chapter 15

Living in a Post-Consumer Economy

Today we'd like to chat with you about the common perception of viewing an economy as a living entity.

For living forms to be considered alive, there are a few character-istics in place: Living forms take in energy and expend energy; living forms have a life span—they are timed to be created and timed to live a life and then disintegrate back into nothing. Living forms also consume—they eat something and, in exchange, expel something else. In the case of the economy being perceived as alive, the health of the economy is based on how much it consumes and grows.

Mind you, growth and consumption are two functions of a living entity, and so if one were to consider an economy as a living entity, then there is nothing wrong per se with that entity's health being based on its consumption and growth. However, there are parts of the equation of a living entity which are missing from a consumer/growth economic model. Therefore,, there is no balance in its model of health. If one is looking at any kind of consumption for any living entity, then one auto-matically knows this: For everything an entity consumes, something is also destroyed. For example, if a human consumes a tomato—the tomato is taken from a tomato vine and then consumed, and it is no more. If an entire plant is harvested, such as a beet and its corresponding greens, and a person consumes that particular plant material, then there is no more beet or greens in existence. It is harvested, and it is also destroyed as a beet plant entity.

Of course, this consumption model does not go just for human living forms but as well for animals of any kind that consume something and it is no longer there: Something is taken in, and its original form is destroyed. You have seen this in your garden this year, yes? Hence, there have been very few flowers in your garden because the deer and an occasional rabbit have considered the garden flowers as food material to be consumed. Again there is no overall judgment against the deer for doing so unless what another entity desires is to have flowers to look at in the garden. Then it is that the deer are seen as a nuisance and are destroying what is desired by another. So, too, if a group of people cast their long nets into a body of water and take out all the fish in water, other living entities will no longer have the benefit of food in that area. And so it goes.

For a very long time, a healthy economy in any given society has been based on consumption without regard to the consequential destruction of or change in something. Growth has been the only way for an economy to be measured as healthy. In other words, if the economy is growing, it is healthy. Conversely, if the economy is shrinking, that is viewed as unhealthy. So in a consumer-based economy, there is no sense of the balance, which all other living entities take into consideration in order to be healthy.

Now, one might argue that an economy is not a living entity. In some people's eyes, that is a silly notion since an economy draws no breath. Yet as you hear every day in your modern media and in your conversations, the economy is perceived as an entity that has a life and is either healthy or ill or ailing or even dying. It can be inflated, akin to being obese and overblown, or deflated, such as a balloon deflates or a mood deflates. Speaking of moods, an economy seems to have emotions as well. It can be depressed, it can be in decline, it can recover, and it can soar.

So therefore, we speak of an economy as you would normally view an economy: as an entity. If there is consumption by an entity with no regard whatsoever to the consequences of that consumption, then eventually you will have an entity usually deemed a monster. An example of one such consumption-oriented entity is cancer. The cells within a cancer consume and grow without regard for its host entity. This unlimited growth has its consequences to the host entity. A consumer-based economy has similar consequences. If an economy is seen as something that needs to grow and consume only—without regard to the consequences of growth and consumption—then there will be a situation where the host entity will eventually suffer from this imbalance just as a host body suffers from the imbalance of a cancer consuming and growing.

For far too long, this imbalanced attitude has held fast: A growing, consuming economy is a healthy one. And when the economy starts to recess, it is seen as a bad thing, even if it is only the Universe's way of rebalancing that which has gone out of control in its growth. Unfortunately for most humans on this planet, there does not seem to be an economy reset button, which one can push in order to bring balance to the economy. No, what usually happens are other forms of balancing take place, commonly known as recessions, crashes, and depressions.

What is also interesting is, similar to a human who is addicted to a certain way of living, it often takes many recessions and crashes in order for human to get the lesson on rebalancing—if they get the lesson at all. Planet-wide, people are addicted to a consumer-based economy and don't even realize it. And so you view the countries that are growing and consuming more and more as emerging economies, while the countries with economies that are already consumption and growth oriented are viewed as strong—until, of course, that system passes and the economy weakens and crashes, much as an addict who no longer has the addicted substance in the body crashes. Can you see why an economy is seen as a living entity?

Perhaps, this is a question that is unanswerable, yet you do not even question this perception—it is the way it is. And so you play your part in the game of feeding and pampering this so-called entity.

As to the future, take comfort in this: In the next few decades, there will be situations where small groups of people will want to create a different way of economic being. We are not suggesting that the old revolutions from your past—such as the communist revolution—will take hold again. We are suggesting that an entirely different view of what an economy is to people's lives will slowly but surely occur.

There will still be a currency for goods and services, as well as an exchange of some sort in the post-consumer economy. There will still be items and foods to consume in this economy. Yet there will also be a sense of balance in this new economy since an important element of life will be taken into consideration, and that is: *What are the consequences of consumption?* A simple enough question, don't you think? As a human body, if you ask, "What are the consequences to my consuming ten cups of sugar to my body?" more than likely you will see consequences that are not to your liking. And so, too, ask questions of consequences to economic behaviors: What are the consequences of creating goods and services of any sort? What energy needs to be expended in order to create those goods or services? How will these actions affect the planet as a whole? How will the creation and consumption of these goods and services affect the groups of people interacting with those goods and services?

A New Point of View

If an economy was seen as an entity that promotes well-being, you would have a distinctively different world. There may still be elements of competition, innovation, consumption, as well as destruction. Yet if the overall goal was to promote well-being of the people and the planet, you would be producing quite different goods and services than the majority of goods and services now available. What we are proposing here is a new way to look at the energy-exchange that is the economy. If it is true that all things are basically energy, then seeing the world economy as an energy exchange rather than as an entity with a moody disposition and an insatiable hunger would immediately bring a radically different perception of living life. Once you start to see the world you inhabit as a constant, non-ending exchange of energy, then many opportunities to live a life of balance will open up for view. However, if you continue to see the world as a world of limitation ruled by a moody entity you call "the economy," you will continue your cyclical, dreary dance of destruction through consumption.

So may we suggest: Put yourself in the center of a world of energy. You're breathing in and exhaling energy. The pressure on certain parts of your body as you sit or stand gives you a sense of the different forms of energy that immediately surround you. What you see with your eyes, taste with your tongue, hear with your ears, and feel with your fingertips gives you a sense of energy variations and exchange. Now expand your awareness to who you are in your home, your neighborhood, your country, the planet, and you can see how much of an integral parcel of energy you become.

Part and parcel of a new economy is considering your part in the whole. What are you consuming? What are you contributing? What are you destroying? What are you creating? What is your energy contributing to the whole in exchange for living in this world? Start with this shift in view, and you will see your life as a human on the planet very differently. Each individual will be working within his or her life's purpose in order to contribute to the whole. Value will be placed on contribution, even if that contribution is only to be here on the planet. Ideas for balance and thriving will be seen as valuable—even more valuable than ideas for defending the structures of an old energy.

View the rest of your day from the perspective of an entity of energy moving in a world of energy. Ask yourself in moments of the day: "What sort of energy am I putting out, and what energy am I consuming?" "How am I contributing to my personal whole as well as to the planetary whole?" "How are my perceptions feeding what I view as my contribution?" and, "What is blocking my ideal of being a healthy contributor to life on the planet?"

Be the blessings you were meant to be, and breathe a new economic reality to life.

That is all for now.

This is the only growth marker that might be lauded and applauded as unending: the growing knowledge of oneself.

Chapter 16

Creating a World You Can
All Live With

*F*orty years from now, looking back, what are things that we're
not seeing that we would benefit from seeing?

You would benefit from remembering that during your historical
reign on this planet, humans have within you both the mechanism for a
conscious awareness of your unity—as well as the continual perception
of separation from each other, from all other beings on the planet, and
from the planet itself. You have both unity awareness and separation
tucked in there as you wander through the forest of your lives.

As you come upon huge and complex challenges, you often get stuck
sitting under a tree in disgust and dismay, thinking that none of this
is ever going to change. Even great leaders who led whole countries or
groupings of people out of the mire of separation and anger needed to
sit under their trees for a while or wander in the wilderness for a time,
lamenting until after a while they'd wonder, "Why am I sitting under
this tree when there is so much to do?" This awareness then pulled
them into action.

The perception of separation is an integral part of life on planet Earth.

Separation is an integral part of your growth towards awareness, towards seeing the bigger picture, towards understanding yourself. As you look back from a viewpoint forty years from now, you will see a pattern of supposed "regression." Temper tantrums will flair. Some will regress to thinking, "We are right, and everyone else is wrong." And some will regress into a survivalist stance and do whatever it takes to maintain an existence, even if the existence is lonely, miserable, and uncomfortable.

Yet the fascinating and incredibly miraculous fact is that these specially-created angels called humans beings are able, with just a slight adjustment of their thinking, to transcend what they thought was hopeless and see possibility in its place. Perceptions are indeed shifting if you look back to this time from forty years hence. Even now, if you look back forty years to see how people saw each other then, it was a very different scene, was it not?

And there was a lot of regression at that time too—and anger and hatred and shaking of fists and arguments and resistance to change. And from that time's perspective, looking forty years back, you might see even more divisiveness; and so on and on, looking back every forty years, you would see drastic changes in attitude, perception, beliefs. You will also see a lot of under-the-tree sitting. You will notice people who are hunkering down, trying to repress the eruption of those who no longer wish to be repressed. You will see tantrums and shouting. These trends come rather naturally to humans.

This particular point in your journey is important to the future of the entire planet's existence, for underlying the surface of all the shouting and screaming and anger and despair, there is a genuine desire for peace, for living with one's neighbor with some sort of equanimity, for drinking clean water, eating clean food, breathing fresh air. You wouldn't know it to look at the headlines of your news outlets; however, it is definitely there and is a much stronger current than it would seem.

In the near-future post-consumer reality, it is not as if people will not consume, yet you will not base your economic health on growth and consumption alone but rather on balance and well-being. Even now, as you consume, you do not personally consume until you explode. Would you do that to yourself? People do not currently take this into consideration, and yet, in this land of so-called freedoms (North America), these are what people consider their basic rights: to consume and consume until they can consume no longer, to trash their own home planet without concern. Until the awakening comes, if they keep up at this pace of consumption, there may be no planet to consume.

So in a post-consumer society, there will be consumption, yes. But there will also be an understanding of the consequences of and limits to consumption.

Your approach to life on the planet will be much more holistic, if we may use that word. You will understand how everyone has a valuable purpose in the great scheme of this Universe—a Universe evolving and growing in its knowledge of itself. This is the only growth marker that might be lauded and applauded as unending: the growing knowledge of oneself. The Universe does this, and you are doing this as well.

Most of you are justifiably angry when you have things you have come to expect taken away from you. We understand this. Yet it is wise to have an understanding of the consequences of growth without limitation. The new prosperity has nothing to do with growing and growing and growing some more. Nor will it be about an accumulation of things. Prosperity will have more to do with working and playing with the flow of energy—sometimes there will be outflow; sometimes there will be inflow, much like the tides.

Forty years hence, for as much as you will allow, people on this diverse planet will be supported in their purpose. People who express their purpose as artists will be supported. People who make sure people are receiving the services they need, or the shelter and food they need, will be supported to do so. The healers will heal, the destroyers will have healthy ways to destroy, and the warriors, too, will have their purpose and place.

Forty years hence, there will be more balance. We are not necessarily talking about nirvana or utopia. The planet is already a paradise of sorts, but it is also a place to play and grow and dream and work with matter and with all the forces of Consciousness. If you desire total oneness at all times, then your desire will bring you to being in spirit and spirit alone—for why would you need to be in separation? If your desire, however, is to be at one with yourself as you are and be at one with all other players as they are, then the place for you is this Earth.

In a post-consumer-driven planet, all this will be taken into consideration: Growth is not the only indicator of health. Consumption is not the only indicator of health. Planetary health requires discernment—an awareness of the consequences of consumption. Planetary health supports each person's prime purpose on the planet. Planetary health requires an awareness of everything's purpose and reason for being.

Live in the physical, yet honor your spiritual presence. Bring out your spiritual presence in whatever way you can. Sometimes no words are needed, just your spirit shining through your human form—that will be enough. At other times, words are needed; explanations are needed; education is needed. In those times, you will be called upon to be an educator of spirit.

In the meantime, celebrate who you are. Shine your light today as much as possible without a need for any feedback and whether you feel you're making a difference or not. Shine anyway. Enough human candles will be lit, and the world will be a brighter place.

And that is all … for now. We'll talk soon.

About the Author:

As a mother of two sons and wife of a brilliant man, these downloads come from my desire to have my own questions answered, and my own fears about the future for my children and loved ones soothed.

I am an ordinary person with an extraordinary gift of seeing energy fields (or auras), and that has provided the back drop to my life's work as a healer and teacher. For 25 years, I've had the privilege to travel the world meeting wonderfully talented people from all walks of life. What I have learned is that no matter what our religious backgrounds, no matter what our spiritual beliefs, most of us worry about the state of the world we inhabit. And most of us wonder, what are we here for?

I am publishing these downloads because their message is of a future we can gift to our children and our children's children. They speak of a wonderful adventure to be lived and cherished. I am truly humbled to be a representative for a Friendly Universe.

Rev. Elke Siller Macartney, Washington State, USA.

www.downloadingafriendlyuniverse.com